Property Rights
Philosophic Foundations

Lawrence C. Becker
Hollins College, Virginia

Routledge & Kegan Paul
London, Henley and Boston

First published in 1977
by Routledge & Kegan Paul Ltd
39 Store Street,
London WC1E 7DD,
Broadway House,
Newtown Road,
Henley-on-Thames,
Oxon RG9 1EN and
9 Park Street,
Boston, Mass. 02108, USA
Set in 10 on 12pt IBM Press Roman by
Express Litho Service (Oxford)
and printed in Great Britain by
Redwood Burn Ltd,
Trowbridge and Esher.

British Library Cataloguing in Publication Data

Becker, Lawrence Carlyle

Property rights.
1. Right of property
I. Title
323.4'6'01   HB701   77-30089

ISBN 0-7100-8679-2

To Charlotte,
to my father, Albert Carlyle Becker,
to my sister Sharyn and brother Michael,
and to the memory of my mother,
Harriette Toren Becker

Contents

Contents

Acknowledgments

I am indebted to many people, and to three institutions, for help with this book. It was written during the academic year 1975-6 when, due to the generous support of the American Council of Learned Societies and the Trustees of Hollins College, I was able to spend the year as a Visiting Fellow in Philosophy at Harvard University. To the associates, tutors, staff and students of Adams House at Harvard — and particularly to the Master of the House, Robert Kiely — I owe special thanks for providing such a pleasant and stimulating environment for work.

Charlotte Becker, Thomas Bergin, Frank Michelman, Robert Nozick, Judith Thomson, and Anthony Woozley read the whole of early drafts and helped me enormously with their comments. Professor Bergin, in particular, stimulated me to make major improvements in the chapter on utility; Professors Nozick and Thomson, along with Professor Ruth Barcan Marcus (who read several of the central chapters), provided the insistent challenges I needed to improve the chapter on the labor theory.

Parts of the manuscript were read at Massachusetts Institute of Technology, North Carolina State University, Yale Law School, and the Eastern Division of the American Philosophical Association at various times during 1975-6. I am indebted to the discussants at those meetings for the help they gave. A short version of chapter 5 was published as 'The Labor Theory of Property Acquisition' in *The Journal of Philosophy,* 73 (1976) pp. 653-4.

No one can doubt, that the convention for the distinction of property, and for the stability of possession, is of all circumstances the most necessary to the establishment of human society, and that after the agreement for the fixing and observing of this rule, there remains little or nothing to be done towards settling a perfect harmony and concord.

David Hume, *Treatise of Human Nature,* book III, part II, §II

The first man who, having enclosed a piece of ground, bethought himself of saying 'This is mine,' and found people simple enough to believe him, was the real founder of civil society. From how many crimes, wars, and murders, from how many horrors and misfortunes might not anyone have saved mankind, by pulling up the stakes, or filling up the ditch, and crying to his fellows: 'Beware of listening to this imposter, you are undone if you once forget that the fruits of the earth belong to us all, and the earth itself to nobody.'

Jean-Jacques Rousseau, *Discourse on Inequality,* part II

1 Introduction

People want their social institutions to be procedurally efficient and fair, to enable the realization of worthy collective and personal goals, to produce results which are just, and to leave them free to pursue whatever activities they themselves choose. Most political philosophy is (among other things) an attempt to work out how deeply inconsistent these wants are, and to decide what can be done about it. This book is no exception.

People who want property want to be left alone to acquire and enjoy it. They want to be able to do what they please with it — to consume it, transform it, exchange it, give it away, put it to good use, or just hold it. How much property people want, what sorts they want, and how much they are willing to let these desires be frustrated in order to achieve other goals varies widely. But a social order must coordinate varying desires if it is to be stable, and the price of stability must be morally justifiable if the social order itself is to be justifiable. The more crowded the planet grows, and the scarcer its resources become, the more difficult this is.

Thoroughgoing libertarians are willing to tolerate nearly any resultant distribution of goods in order to preserve the liberties of a social order based on private ownership. Socialists are willing to restrict or eliminate almost any form of private ownership in order to achieve justice in distribution. But it has become increasingly evident over the last century that advocates of a compromise between libertarian and socialist extremes lack a principled consensus about what they will or will not tolerate. My object here is to make a contribution toward such a principled consensus.

In particular, I shall argue against anti-property theorists that private property rights, while not natural rights in any meaningful sense, are

1

none the less justifiable by several independent lines of argument. Indeed, I shall urge that within certain significant constraints, people ought to be free to acquire and keep whatever and as much as they want. Against libertarians, however, I shall argue that there *are* significant constraints on legitimate acquisition and ownership rights, that these constraints become increasingly stringent as scarcity increases, and that we now need redefinitions of the sorts of private ownership rights we allow. Finally, against the zeal of some reformers and some legal theorists who discuss the law of 'takings,' I shall argue that any overriding of an existing property right must either be with the right-holder's consent or else be accompanied by just compensation. In consequence, where just compensation is impossible, and consent cannot be obtained, no overriding of the right is justifiable.

Taken separately, these conclusions are not novel (however distressing they may be to some), and they are not very specific about details. I hope to make up for such shortcomings by the soundness and comprehensiveness of the arguments I present. But my concern is, after all, with the philosophic foundations, not the legal superstructure. The effort is to place discussion of the details firmly into a comprehensive and clear statement of justificatory premises: into a comprehensive statement because philosophers have too often pushed their points as partisans for a particular brand of moral theory, ignoring sound arguments from other sources; into a clear statement because property theorists have too often operated with nothing more than an attractive metaphor as a starting point — a metaphor whose use, on inspection, is neither capable of coherent explication nor amenable to rational justification. The arguments here will be, in short, philosophic.

The need for a new theory

Philosophizing about property used to be risky. The history of property acquisition is a sordid one — examples of honest effort notwithstanding — and inequity in the distribution of goods has always been visible. An institution which has had to manage the results of so much injustice, and which has so often been used to perpetuate inequity, has an understandable aversion to moral analysis. Or perhaps more accurately, people who want their possessions protected as property are often hostile to attempts to find out whether what they want is morally justifiable. In uncivilized times, such hostility can be expressed in uncivilized ways.

This has not been lost on philosophers. Those who have defended private property have written soberly — casting whatever reservations they may have had into thickets which the propertied reader could avoid. Those who have attacked private property have usually shown the signs of intense frustration — rage, hyperbole, and despair at achieving any reform by rational persuasion. Reasoned argument, when it comes in conflict with the desire to get and keep something, is grossly overmatched.

The riskiness of writing about property has largely disappeared. The problem now is whether there is any longer any point in doing so. The main lines of argument for the general justification of property have long since been laid down; the vulnerable areas in those justifications have been identified; alternatives to private ownership have been proposed; weaknesses in those proposals have been explored. It seems unlikely that any new discussion could make a significant contribution to theory. And it seems even less likely that it could have significant practical consequences. The changes in property rights which have occurred in the last six or seven decades — and those which will doubtless occur in the next six or seven — are startling, to say the least. But they have not — nor are they likely to begin to — come about as the result of a clear and comprehensive new theory of property. The modern industrial state is so complex, its basic institutions so entrenched and interdependent, that basic changes come about more by the accidental confluence of particular interests than by design. The action guidance moral philosophy might provide thus seems a bit beside the point.

Yet property rights badly need philosophical discussion. Traditional philosophical arguments for and against various forms of property are seriously flawed. They are based on naive or hasty analyses of the concept of rights *per se* and property rights in particular. They rarely prove what they say they prove (a fact noticed by all their critics), but they often do prove some other interesting things (things their critics overlook). They usually address themselves to the question farthest removed from practical concerns — namely why there should ever be any property rights at all; what I call the problem of *general* justification. They consequently slight the most important question — namely what sorts of people should own what sorts of things and under what conditions; the problem of *specific* justification. Most damaging of all, they are each typically embedded in a general moral theory which makes it difficult to use one argument to support, augment, or restrict another. Utilitarians scorn claims founded on justice in original acquisition; advocates of the labor theory are reluctant to limit the claims of justice by weighing in the consequences for the promotion of good (as opposed to the demotion of evil); and the defenders of 'ownership by the property worthy' largely ignore both utility and the labor theory. Thus divided against themselves, the arguments for property rights are easy prey. At a minimum, the traditional arguments need to be re-examined and their results coordinated into a coherent theory.

Further, from a practical point of view, the existence of a sound, clear, and thorough philosophic analysis of the general theory of property rights would be useful. Changes in ownership rights are usually made piecemeal: zoning ordinances are passed; acquisition and use of water is controlled; new forms of wealth emerge; and as quickly as one form of taxation is instituted, ways of avoiding it are invented. Existing overviews of what sorts of property rights people ought to have are either simplistic visions of an ideal world (e.g. Edward Bellamy; Ayn Rand), political polemics (Proudhon; some of Marx), or tunnel-visioned defenses of the *status quo* or an *idée fixe* (Locke; the rest of Marx; Mill). Sober, practical people who are trying to make the system work have to operate either with these existing materials, unfortunately hardened into political ideologies, or with a confusing and largely incoherent set of intuitions amounting to little more than this: that people are entitled to the produce of their labor; that they ought to have the liberty to acquire things by their labor; that there is *something* (it is unclear just what) true about the claim that 'first in time is first in right'; that things ought to be owned by the people who can and will use them properly; and that somehow, all of this has to be controlled by the principles of utility. In the face of this, it is not surprising that changes in ownership rights are made somewhat haphazardly. Philosophers should be able to provide a better foundation for practice than now exists.

Foundations for a new theory

And they can. The foundations for a new theory of property rights – a theory which is independent of the rigidity and ultimate mystery of seventeenth-century natural rights theory, as well as of the ruthlessly forward-looking concerns of utilitarian and revolutionary socialist theories – can be laid by a careful analysis of the relevant distinctions with regard to rights *per se*, property rights in particular, and the concept of the justification of a property right, together with an equally careful assessment of the traditional arguments for and against private property. By doing these things, this book aims to clear the way for a sustained, detailed, and coherent theory of the specific sorts of property rights people ought to have. Its object is thus to lay the foundations for a new theory of property.

The foundations I propose are not easily labelled. They are not extracted from a central, illuminating metaphor (like the Lockean mixing of one's labor with things); nor are they easily categorizable as an 'ism'. Rather, they consist in the results of my arguments on the whole range of illuminating metaphors and 'isms' which have traditionally been used to found theories of property rights. Specifically, I shall argue in what follows:

(1) for specific conceptions of the central notions of rights in general, property rights in particular, and what it is to justify a property right;

(2) for specific interpretations of traditional arguments for and against property rights – i.e. the arguments from first occupancy, labor, utility, liberty, and virtue or property worthiness;

(3) that out of all this there are only four sound lines of justification for the institution of private property rights – one from utility; one from liberty; and two from the labor theory;

(4) that any attempt to justify a particular sort of property right (e.g. unrestricted ownership of land) must be compatible with these general lines of justification – that is, be bound by any limitations they impose on all ownership;

(5) that these lines of justification, together with what is sound in the standard anti-property arguments, impose severe restrictions upon the sorts of property rights which can today be justified – particularly with respect to ownership of scarce resources and the right to bequeath one's property; and

(6) in particular, I shall argue (a) that private ownership of land, water, fossil fuels, and mineral deposits – as generally defined in the Western democracies – must now be redefined; (b) that accumulations of wealth which tend to undermine democratic political processes must be controlled; and (c) that within the limits imposed by general justifying conditions, systems of property rights must allow as much acquisition as individuals want.

I do not pretend to say all that should be said on these topics. I do, however, hope to say enough to give a sound foundation to a much-needed new theory. My conclusions on these six topics constitute that foundation. They are a foundation in the sense that they establish the points in the moral landscape upon which an institution of property rights can rest, and an outline for the definition of such an institution. But they are *only* a foundation: they define the limits of size and shape; they do not specify the details. Those details, the real substance of any theory of property rights, are in many instances very complex. Water rights, land rights, the rights of bequest and the other substantive elements of a specific theory, require separate treatment.

Private property and property rights *per se*

While some of what follows will be applicable to a discussion of property rights *per se* — that is, to systems of state or communal ownership as well as to systems of private ownership — it should be kept in mind that the primary aim here is the analysis of arguments for private property. Of course the discussion of the very *concept* of a property right applies across the board, and some arguments (notably those from utility) will justify a system of state or communal ownership in cases where they fail to justify private property. But again, the purpose here is to discuss the justifiability of private property. Having given this notice, I shall often drop the modifier 'private' in what follows. The context should always make clear what is meant.

Scarcity

As a final introductory note, it should be mentioned that the scarcity of goods is regarded by most writers as the central, controlling fact of the contexts in which problems about property rights arise. Indeed, many writers on property feel obliged to begin with remarks to the effect that, were it not for scarcity, there would be no need for the institution of ownership. There is, of course, a good deal of truth in this. Even if a good is not now actually scarce, its ownership can be problematic to the extent that the good can *become* scarce — e.g. by being used up or by being controlled by a few people. And if a good were to be inexhaustible and unlimitedly available to all, it is difficult to imagine that much of importance could hang on who owned what parts of it.

But like many seemingly obvious general pronouncements, it is not so clear, upon inspection, that this one is as uncontestable as it seems. If it is the case, as some defenders of property have supposed, that appropriating things is an essential part of the full development of a human personality, then it is not necessarily true that the elimination of scarcity eliminates the problems which call for a theory of property rights. For it may be, then, that the preservation (through a system of property rights) of one's possessions has some importance just because those things are one's own appropriations — regardless of whether or not they are scarce or likely to become scarce. I have therefore chosen not to make the usual deep bow to the notion of scarcity.

2 Property Rights

This chapter presents an analytical apparatus which is important for the sake of clarity and economy in the arguments to follow, but which is uncontroversial for present purposes. Those who are already familiar with its fundamentals will therefore not need to read the chapter closely. Mastery of the Hohfeldian definitions of 'rights,' 'privileges,' 'powers,' and 'immunities' (here claim rights, liberties, powers, and immunities) is important, however, as is familiarity with A. M. Honoré's analysis of the full or liberal concept of ownership. These things are summarized on pages 11-15 and 18-20, respectively. Readers who skip the review of Hohfeld should at least consult the discussion of 'recipient rights' on pages 14-15. All readers should note the remarks on the justification of property rights on pages 22-3.

Rights

'Right' has multiple meanings, and they are so deeply entrenched in both ordinary and technical usages that the best one can hope for is to keep the various meanings distinct and see to it that the distinctions are attended to. Discussions of property rights are often damaged by careless use of terms like 'natural' or 'human' rights, vagueness in distinguishing moral from legal rights, and an imprecise understanding of the root idea of a right. What I want to do here, as a prelude to discussing the complexity of the concept of a property right, is to state with some care what I take to be the root idea of a right, and then explicate the elements of that root idea. I shall argue that all the sorts of rights philosophers find it necessary to distinguish can be given adequately precise definitions by reference to those elements.

THE ROOT IDEA OF A RIGHT

When moral philosophers contrast rights with ideals, rights with personal or social goods, or rights with virtues, what they mean by 'right' seems to be something like this:

> The existence of a right is the existence of a state of affairs in which one person (the right-holder) has a claim on an act or forbearance from another person (the duty-bearer) in the sense that, should the claim be exercised or in force, and the act or forbearance not be done, it would be justifiable, other things being equal, to use coercive measures to extract either the performance required or compensation in lieu of that performance.

(Occasionally, both performance and compensation are extracted, or alternatively, both compensatory and punitive damages. This translates, in 'friendly' situations, into performance or compensation plus apology.)

The leading characteristics of a right defined in this way are its correlation with the notion of duty, its involvement with coercion, the fact that it may be concerned with either acts or omissions, and the fact that violations require restitution. But it is just these characteristics (plus a few others) which quickly bring the definition under criticism. Must all right-holders be persons? (What about corporations? Animals? Trees?) Must all rights entail correlative duties? Are some rights always 'in force'? What sort of coercion is permissible and who may exercise it? When is compensation an adequate remedy?

Questions like these generate the bewildering variety of attempts to classify rights — to define various types. And I think the most perspicuous overview of the concept of a right comes from a consideration of the various ways these questions can be answered. The following elements of the root idea of a right raise the relevant questions.

ELEMENTS IN THE ANALYSIS OF A RIGHT

(1) *Specification of the right-holders.* Generally speaking, who may be a right-holder is decided by the filling in of items (3), (4), and (5) below — and that includes questions about whether animals, trees, and future generations have rights. Element (3), the general nature of the right-relationship between the holder and others, will clearly be partly determinative. If the right-holder is said to possess the power intentionally to alter, at will, some of the rights-relationships of others, then that clearly restricts the class of right-holders to individuals who have the capacity to act 'at will.' Element (4), the 'content' of the right, is further determinative. If the right-holder is entitled to abortion on demand, one assumes that the class of right-holders is limited to those individuals who have the capacities to be pregnant and to demand abortions. And element (5), the specification of the conditions under

which a right-claim may be said to be valid, also helps to specify right-holders. If a line of argument used to establish the legitimacy of a certain sort of right-claim only applies to humans, or to children, or to wild animals, then the class of right-holders is similarly circumscribed. (One parenthetical remark. I suppose it is true that, as ordinarily understood, a right-holder may be either an individual [human or not] or an institution. A mere aggregate of individuals should probably not be regarded as a holder of rights. At least, it is hard to think of a case in which one would have to consider the question of the rights of an aggregate distinct from the question of the rights of its members, considered as individuals. But institutions may be somewhat different. Landowning corporations have certain rights with regard to their land which may be exercised by individuals acting for the corporation, but which cannot really be said to be held, except in a derivative sense, by any individual.)

(2) *Specification of the right-regarders.* Those who must 'observe' or 'respect' or 'honor' the right may similarly be individuals or institutions (i.e. individuals acting through or on behalf of institutions, carrying out the activities of members or officers of institutions). I suspect there is general agreement that in moral contexts right-regarders must be 'persons' (human or not), but that again is determined by the filling in of items (3), (4), and (5) below.

(3) *The specification of general nature of the relation between right-holders and right-regarders.* Hohfeld distinguished four general sorts of relation between holders and regarders: right/duty relations; privilege/no-right relations; power/liability relations; and immunity/disability relations.[1] I shall suggest later that there are others, but that will require some argument. (If there is some perplexity about what distinguishes the 'general' nature of the rights-relationship from other elements of its nature, it will suffice for present purposes simply to think of this category as a left-over. The general nature is whatever of importance is not specified by the other nine elements in this list.)

(4) *The specification of the act, forbearance, status, or benefit 'owed' to or possessed by the right-holder.* This element, which concerns what might be called the 'content' of the right, may be filled in with something very abstract (free speech) or very concrete (the delivery, by 26 April 1979, of $40,000 in cash). It becomes a particularly vexing problem when the thing specified is not determinate — e.g. health care. Is a right to health care to mean that one has a right to treatment by the best medical professionals with the best equipment? A right to as much as one wants? Needs?

(5) *The specification of the conditions under which a right-claim may*

be said to be sound. This involves the specification of *general* justifying conditions (the things which justify any right-claims at all, ever), *specific* justifying conditions (the things which, given the general justifying conditions, justify the *sort* of right-claim at issue), and *particular* justifying conditions (the things which, given the general and specific justifying conditions, justify the particular right-claim at issue).

(6) *Specification of the conditions under which a right may be said to have been violated.* Here are two distinct issues. First, when has a right-regarder failed to fulfill the right-claim? Some rights lie fallow, as it were, until specifically 'exercised' by the right-holder, and if they are not exercised, they cannot be violated. Other rights are perpetually 'in force.' Further, some rights are specific as to when their claims must be met; others are not. In the latter case, when does one say that a right-regarder has failed to meet the claim (as opposed to saying that he or she has simply not *yet* met it)?

Second, one must specify, for each right, the conditions under which it may be justifiably overriden. Overriding a right is to be distinguished from violating it. The distinction will be drawn, naturally enough, by derivation from the three filled-in sets of justifying conditions listed under (5) above as they relate to the justifications for conflicting moral values, duties, or virtues.

(7) *Specification of the conditions under which the violation of a right is excusable.* This involves the determination of (a) the general criteria for judging an agent responsible for her or his acts; and (b) any circumstances special to the particular case which make the imposition of sanction either pointless or as great or greater an injustice than the original violation of right.

(8) *Specification of the appropriate remedies.* These will vary, for one thing, with respect to whether a right has been (justifiably) overriden, inexcusably or excusably violated. For the first and third categories punitive damages are ruled out by definition (justification and excuse entail non-culpability and hence the injustice of any specifically punitive sanction). But compensation is not ruled out in such cases; indeed, it may be required.

The appropriateness of a remedy in all three categories is determined by the relevant requirements of compensatory and retaliatory justice. It should be noted, however, that it may be that once some rights (e.g. the right to life) have been violated, neither restitution nor compensation in lieu of it is logically possible. And in other cases (the right-holder's loss of a limb), compensation is a paltry substitute for restitution.

(9) *Specification of the methods to be used in extracting the remedies.* These also may be said to derive from the requirements of compensatory and retaliatory justice, as controlled by rights which remain in the

wrongdoer, as well as by considerations of utility. An important consideration in any society with a legal system is whether the right is to be legally enforced.

(10) *Specification of the agent(s) who may extract the remedies.* Here there may be rules barring third parties, or barring the victim, or requiring some 'official' be the one who extracts the remedies.

These, then, are the elements in terms of which the root idea of a right may be analyzed. I want to show now that one can organize various typologies of rights simply by paying attention to the ways these elements are filled in. Specifically, I want to show how much of an overview of the whole concept of rights can be gotten by first considering element (3), the general nature of the relationship between a right-holder and others, then element (5), the conditions which justify right-claims. I will propose schematic definitions for most of the major sorts of rights commonly distinguished. The definitions themselves (though I think they are good ones) may be arguable. What I hope is not arguable is the usefulness of this *method* of defining rights.

TYPES OF RIGHTS-RELATIONSHIPS

Perhaps the most crucial set of distinctions to be made involves element (3), the general nature of the relations between right-holders and others. As already noted, Hohfeld distinguished four important kinds of rights with regard to this element,[2] and while I think his list is not complete, at least for moral purposes, I shall begin by reviewing it.[3]

Claim-right (or right in the strict sense).[4] Here the existence of a right may be characterized almost exactly as was the root idea of a right. It is the existence of a state of affairs such that one individual or institution (the right-holder) has a claim on another (the duty-bearer) for an act or forbearance in the sense that, should the claim be in force or exercised, and the act or forbearance not done, it would be moral (or legal, in the case of a legal right), other things being equal, to use coercive measures to extract either the specific performance (i.e. the act or forbearance claimed), or compensation in lieu of it.

The existence of a claim right in one person entails the existence of a duty in another. 'Having a duty,' as used here, may be defined as being required to perform an act or forbearance in the sense that, should the requirement be in force, and the act or forbearance not done, it would be moral (or legal) for others to use coercive measures to extract either the specific performance required or compensation in lieu of it.

There are, of course, many sorts of claim rights which can be distinguished. One may wish to separate duties to *act* (which correlate with 'positive' claim rights), from duties to *forbear* (which correlate with 'negative' claim rights). One may wish to separate the claim rights held against individuals from those held against institutions. And one may wish to separate those for whose violation performance alone is an adequate remedy from those for whose violation either performance or compensation will suffice. When references to other elements of the schema are added (e.g. who may hold the rights, who may enforce them), it is easy to distinguish a great variety of types. Most of the possibilities are straightforward enough not to need comment.

There is, however, one special sort of claim right which has been the source of enough confusion to warrant special treatment.[5] The sort I have in mind may be called a *capacity-claim*, and may be described as follows: One may wish, in asserting one's rights, to call particular attention to one's status as a potential *holder* of rights. That is, one may wish merely to assert, with a statement such as 'I have a right to get married,' that one is of age and mentally competent – that one has the legal capacity to get married.

This sort of claim right easily causes confusion, because the relevant 'capacity' or 'standing' is presupposed by the existence of other sorts of rights. Having a right to score a goal in a soccer game is part liberty (no one has a right that you not score) and part power (if you do put the ball in the net in the prescribed manner, your goal must be recognized), but both parts of the right presuppose that you are a player – that is, that you have the requisite capacity or standing to exercise the liberty/ power right to score. Thus, when one asserts the right to score (meaning the liberty/power right) one also necessarily presupposes that one has the requisite capacity. *But when the existence of that capacity is itself at issue,* one may want to 'back up' as it were and assert *it* alone. Right-claim locutions come naturally here, they amount to the assertion that others 'owe' one the recognition that one has the capacity – the relevant qualifications or standing as defined by the right-making institutions or considerations – to possess one or more sorts of rights.

The existence of the (legal or moral) capacity to possess rights, then, in the sense that its recognition is owed the person having it, is the existence of a capacity-claim right. I regard this as a claim right because correlative duty-bearers can be specified, and the remedy for violations (failure to recognize• capacity-claims) is the extraction of the performance (the recognition) from the duty-bearer.

Liberty.[6] Not all rights, however, entail the existence of duties in others. For example, we may say that one person (the right-holder) is at liberty with respect to some others to do or not to do a given thing. The others have no claim right against the right-holder, either to the effect that the thing *not* be done, or that it *be* done. And the right-holder has no duty either to do it or not to do it. Competitive situations provide good examples. Competitors have claim rights and duties with respect to fair play, the rules of the game, and so forth. But each is *at liberty* to win ('has a right to win'). No one has a duty to win, or to let another win.

The existence of a liberty right in one entails only the *absence* of claim rights in others. It does not entail the existence of duties. What confuses the situation is that liberties are often secured by claim rights — especially for forbearance from others. Thus my liberty to speak freely may be given legal emphasis by the enforcement of certain duties in others not to interfere with my exercise of that liberty. But claim rights and liberty rights are none the less distinct in principle.

As with claim rights, there are important distinctions which can be made among liberties. For example, there are what might be called *natural* as opposed to *derived* (or institutional) liberties. The former are the sort which can exist independently of any social institutions. Human beings in the proverbial state of nature have complete natural liberty — i.e. no one has any claim rights against them for the performance or nonperformance of any act. Once political or social institutions arise, natural liberties are limited (though many may remain), but political and social liberties of various sorts become possible. That is, one can then speak of liberties whose existence is logically dependent on the existence of political or social institutions — *derived* or *institutional* liberties. Examples are one's liberty to win a game. Until games exist, the liberty to win can not logically exist. (The attempt to prove the moral necessity of some system of political liberty from the characteristics of complete natural liberty — together with certain other features of the human condition — has been one of the great projects of social-contract theory.)

Power. A third type of relationship between right-holders and others is what Hohfeld labelled a power. My right to make a will is the legal (and perhaps moral) ability to alter my relations to others (with respect to rights). That is, the existence of a power right is the existence of a state of affairs such that one person (the right-holder) may morally (or legally) alter at will some of the rights, duties, liberties, powers, or immunities of another person (the liability-bearer). The existence of a power right entails only liability in others — that is, the fact that certain of their rights-relationships are subject to alteration by the power-holder. Power rights, like liberty rights, are often given effectiveness by strategically placed duties and claim rights.

It is important to notice, here, that powers may be either perfect or imperfect. That is, they may be such that the power-holder can *alone*

13

alter the rights-relationships of others, or they may be such that the power-holder can only do so with the participation of others. Hohfeld recognized this distinction,[7] but did not dwell on it, and I think it is important enough to warrant some separate attention. In fact a cursory survey of power rights will reveal that what I shall call *participant-powers* are the rule rather than the exception.

Example: a priest has the right to marry people, but this does not mean that he can do so at will — that is, that unmarried people have a corresponding liability to have their marital status altered at the priest's discretion. The right to enter into bilateral contracts is similar. One is not just at liberty to do such things, nor does one simply have the power to do them. It is, rather, impossible (perhaps for logical, or legal, or moral reasons) to do these things by oneself — one can only *partici-pate* in them as joint enterprises. Hence something is missed by merely saying that a person is at liberty to make bilateral contracts in the sense that no one has a right against that person that he or she not make them. And the situation is even more seriously misdescribed by simply saying that the person has the *power, simpliciter*, to contract or perform a wedding. It is rather the case that people have the right to *participate* in these events in the sense that certain of their efforts, when joined with those of other people, can alter legal or moral rights-relationships.

I shall say that the existence of such a state of affairs is the existence of a participant-power. And it is clear that this is an important subclass of rights-relationships, both for the law and for morality. It is intimately involved with the definition of offices and roles.

Immunity. Hohfeld's fourth type of right-relationship refers to a state of affairs in which one person (the right-holder) is not under a liability with respect to the power of another — that is, is not subject to the other's altering, at will, his or her rights-relationships. The existence of an immunity in one entails a *disability* in another. Like liberties and powers, immunities are often reinforced with claim rights.

Recipient rights. In addition to Hohfeld's four kinds of rights-relationships, even as augmented with the subclasses I have listed, philosophers have occasionally found it important to speak of another kind — one which has some of the stringency of a claim right (the right-holder is 'owed' or 'entitled' to something) but for which no corresponding duty-bearers can be specified. For example, suppose it is claimed that every adult pregnant woman has a right to have an abortion if she wants one, and that that right is more than a mere liberty. (It is not self-induced abortion we are talking about, but properly performed, medical abortion. To say that a woman has a right to an abortion if she wants one, then, is to say that she is owed the necessary *services*.) We may be prepared to impose the correlative duties on medical professionals. If so, the right to an abortion is a straightforward claim right. But suppose we are not? Suppose we want to assert that every woman has a right to (is somehow owed) an abortion if she wants one, but we are *not* prepared to impose a duty on all or any particular medical professionals to provide the service. (This is very nearly an accurate description of the current situation in the United States.) Such rights stand midway, as it were, between claim rights and liberties; they may be considered to be 'imperfect' claim rights, or 'augmented' liberties. In any case their status is problematic, particularly for the law, because, though they assert that something is owed the right-holder, their failure to specify who should 'pay' renders them unenforceable. They are, rather, simply assertions that (a) some person (the right-holder, is owed or entitled to something in the sense that (b) if it is obtained, the recipient need not accept it with the gratitude appropriate to the receipt of a gift, but may (properly) accept it as one would accept the honoring of a claim right; and (c) if it is not obtained, the right-holder may appropriately respond as if an (unspecifiable) duty-bearer had violated a claim right.

I shall call the existence of this state of affairs the existence of a recipient right.[8] It is an important and interesting sort of moral claim,[9] but one which often leads to confusion. People who have in effect persuaded themselves that such a right (say to health care) exists, often assume that it has — or must quickly be upgraded to — the status of a claim right. Others, recognizing only the conventional Hohfeldian categories of rights-relationships, assume that because a correlative duty-bearer cannot be specified, no 'real' right exists. Discussion then quickly degenerates.

Claim rights (including capacity-claims), liberties, powers (including participant powers), immunities, and recipient rights are all typed, then, by reference to the general sort of relationship that exists between the right-holder and others — that is, they are distinguished from one another primarily by how element (3) in the schema is filled in.

TYPES OF RIGHTS BY SOURCE OF JUSTIFICATION

I want to conclude this overview of the concept of a right with a final set of examples which center on the filling in of element (5), the specification of the conditions under which a right-claim may be said to be justified. This element, as supplemented with some others, figures heavily in the definition of many of the types of rights moral philosophers distinguish.

For example, a *natural right* is one which arises from conditions (as in element (5)) which may, in some plausible sense, be said to 'occur naturally.' The notion of a natural right is primarily designed to mark the distinction between rights which arise from human institutions — particularly from practices intentionally designed to be right-making — and rights which 'just exist.' Rights which arise because people make agreements with each other or because they accept the rule of law, or the rules of a particular institution, are *not* examples of natural rights; they are ordinarily called *conventional* or *special* rights. Rights which are justified in terms of the minimum requirements for social stability, or human dignity, are natural rights — even if the list of minimum requirements is heavily influenced by the particular set of institutions humans have created. The distinction is not a perfectly sharp one, but it is clear that it is to be made in terms of the fifth element of the analysis.

A *human right* is (oversimply) either a natural or a conventional right held by all and only human beings. (A right to the same thing, held by Martians, is then a Martian right.) The qualifier 'human' here only restricts the scope of right-holders (element (1)). The conditions under which the holder's claim may be said to be sound are the same as those for other rights (except that they specify the whole class of human beings as the only right-holders).

Legal rights are those which 'are' matters of law in a given system. I put 'are' in scare quotes to indicate a problem; one's theory of law will determine, in each case, *what* rights are matters of law. Oversimply, for a legal realist, legal rights are those which the courts will in fact enforce. For a modern positivist, they are those 'recognized,' implicitly or explicitly, by the legal system. For the natural-law theorist, they are the ones the system *ought* to recognize. Here again the primary distinguishing mark is the filling in of element (5) — the conditions under which a right claim may be said to be justified. But of course the definition is also concerned with elements (8), (9), and (10) — the specification of appropriate remedies, coercive measures, and agents who may carry them out. A given legal system may (but need not in principle) limit the sorts of right-relationships (under element (3)) which it recognizes.

Private (legal) rights are legal rights distinguished by reference to element (1) — who may be a right-holder. In this case, that means individuals in their 'non-official' and 'non-affiliated' capacities (though citizenship can be a prerequisite). With the suitable modifications, one can have categories of private rights which are natural, special, human, or moral.

Civil rights are private, legal rights. But in addition to that, civil rights are distinguished by reference to the entities against whom the rights are held. Although civil rights are rights against individuals (any individuals specified by law), they are also *rights against the state*. It is this feature, and not their content under item (4), which primarily distinguishes them from other private legal rights. (A list of civil rights now recognized in the United States might well show some unifying elements of content. It seems to me that any such unity is purely a contingent matter, however.)

Primary and *secondary rights* are sometimes distinguished. A secondary right is one which is entailed by the existence of another right, and is extinguished when the primary right is extinguished. Thus the distinction is clearly to be drawn in terms of element (5).

Moral rights are, I think, best distinguished from other sorts of rights by the filling in of elements (5) and (10) primarily – that is, the conditions which establish or justify claims for their existence, and the specification of who may enforce them. It has been argued by Hart[10] that what I list as items (7), (8), and (9) – that is, the specification of excusing conditions, appropriate remedies, and methods used to extract the remedies – are also relevant to distinguishing moral from legal obligations (and, *ipso facto,* moral from legal rights), but he recognizes exceptions in each of these cases (e.g. moral obligations are typically – but not always – less 'physically' enforced than legal ones). So I suggest that the distinction is best drawn by reference to the sort of conditions which can generate the right, and the sort of agents who are to enforce the rights. After that has been done, it may be appropriate to comment on tendencies to differ on items (7), (8), and (9).

It is important to notice, however, that one's concept of morality will be as crucial here as one's concept of law is in determining what counts as a legal right. If references to prudence, utility, and the interests and desires of the moral agent are *excluded* from moral argument – that is, not regarded as *moral* reasons, reasons which could justify a course of conduct as a *moral* one – then the notion of a moral right will be similarly restricted. But if moral argument is regarded as the most general category of practical discourse – an 'all things considered' form of argument – the notion of a moral right will look very different. In any case, it is clear that moral rights can also be private or not, legal or not, natural, human, or special, primary or secondary. They can also involve any one or any combination of the rights-relationships described as claims, liberties, powers, immunities, and recipient rights.

One could go on along these lines for a very long time. One could argue about variant definitions of the types of rights already mentioned; and one could go on to define the many other sorts of rights which are distinguished for special purposes (e.g. perfect and imperfect, positive and negative, *in rem* and *in personam*, proprietary and personal, vested and contingent rights). But I think it is clear that these too can be defined (perhaps in more than one way) by reference to the ten elements of the root idea of a right.

Since my purpose here was only to give an overview of the concept of a right — a perspicuous schema for defining and understanding the interrelations of various types of rights — I shall not go on to define more types or to argue for the schematic definitions already given. Enough has been said, I think, to make my point: that the sorely needed overview of the concept of a right can be obtained by focusing first on the elements of the root idea of a right, and then defining various types of rights by the ways in which those elements are defined. I want now to turn to the concept of a property right, a concept whose complexity has too often been ignored — to the detriment of philosophical discussions of property.

Property rights

Property rights, as I shall use the term, are the rights of ownership.[11] But 'the rights of ownership' is not an unequivocal term. It is clear enough that ownership typically has something to do with the right to use, the right to transfer, and the right to exclude others from the thing owned. And most philosophical discussions of property content themselves with this broad characterization, noting in passing that certain restrictions (e.g. prohibition of harmful use) and extensions (e.g. the right to bequeath) are usually associated with it.[12] But the right of use is itself a bundle of rights which mature legal systems separate, and when the other elements of legal ownership are examined, it quickly becomes obvious that a person may own things (legally) in a variety of overlapping but quite distinct senses. Philosophical discussion will profit from a consideration of legal analyses of the concept.

FULL OWNERSHIP

A. M. Honoré has given a particularly lucid account of the 'full' or 'liberal' concept of ownership — a concept he says is common to all 'mature' legal systems.[13] A summary of his list of the elements ('legal incidents') which make up the concept is a convenient place to begin.

Honoré maintains that the full or liberal notion of ownership (though it is, of course, subject to other analyses) is most adequately explicated by reference to the following list of elements.

(1) *The right to possess* – that is, to exclusive physical control of the thing owned. Where the thing cannot be possessed physically, due, for example, to its 'non-corporeal' nature, 'possession' may be understood metaphorically or simply as the right to exclude others from the use or other benefits of the thing.

(2) *The right to use* – that is, to personal enjoyment and use of the thing as distinct from (3) and (4) below.

(3) *The right to manage* – that is, to decide how and by whom a thing shall be used.

(4) *The right to the income* – that is, to the benefits derived from foregoing personal use of a thing and allowing others to use it.

(5) *The right to the capital* – that is, the power to alienate the thing and to consume, waste, modify, or destroy it.

(6) *The right to security* – that is, immunity from expropriation.

(7) *The power of transmissibility* – that is, the power to devise or bequeath the thing.

(8) *The absence of term* – that is, the indeterminate length of one's ownership rights.

(9) *The prohibition of harmful use* – that is, one's duty to forbear from using the thing in certain ways harmful to others.

(10) *Liability to execution* – that is, liability to having the thing taken away for repayment of a debt.

(11) *Residuary character* – that is, the existence of rules governing the reversion of lapsed ownership rights.

Honoré is quick to point out that although all of the eleven incidents are necessary for full or liberal ownership as defined by existing mature legal systems, none of them is a necessary constitutent of ownership *per se*, for people may be said to own things in various restricted senses which omit any one or more of the incidents. One might, for example, have the right to the income of one's trust, but not the right to its capital or management. Or one might have the right to management and income of one's house, but (due to leasing agreements) only restricted rights to use, possession, and capital.

Further, each of the incidents is susceptible of varying definitions – not, perhaps, enough to alter its general idea, but enough to alter emphasis and practical consequences. Transmissibility, for example, is usually defined so as to exclude perpetuities. Harmful use may shade into a requirement for productive use. The right to income may be defined to permit taxation. The right to security may be defined to permit state expropriation under certain circumstances. And so forth.

Finally, the incidents are susceptible of differing scopes. There may be restrictions on what one can own in various senses: e.g. in the case of land as opposed to chattels, a legal system could restrict ownership to the rights of life-tenancy, use, management, and income, excluding the right to the capital or the power of transmissibility.

VARIETIES OF OWNERSHIP

Just as there is no single definition of ownership in a given legal system, so there is no single definition of full or liberal ownership among legal systems. The list of elements may be standard (Honoré says it is), but the definition and scope given to each is subject to significant variations. Nevertheless, for the purposes of the discussion to follow, it will be useful to specify the subsets of Honoré's list which it seems reasonable to regard as varieties of ownership, leaving aside, for now, issues of the precise definition and scope of each subset.

I suggest (on the basis of nothing stronger than a feel for the semantic proprieties) that the following subsets of the eleven elements each constitute a variety of what may reasonably be called ownership.

The right to the capital is the only one of the elements which seems able to define a variety of ownership standing alone. It is the most fundamental of the elements, if only because it includes the right to destroy, consume, and alienate. (Alienation is understood to include exchanges, gifts, and just 'letting go.') This makes absence of term rather academic, and the other incidents can be seen as protections, extensions, restrictions, or elaborations of this right. One who has all the rights in the list save that of capital may own the thing in a derivative sense, but the one who has the right to the capital is 'fundamentally' the owner.

It follows that, if the right to capital is enough, by itself, to claim ownership, any subset of elements which includes it will also be sufficient for the claim. Of course, a suitably strong prohibition of harmful use, or a whimsically short term, or a sweeping allowance of expropriation may effectively destroy the right to capital, but then the element is in effect absent from the subset.

The right to security in possession, security in use, security in management,[14] and security in income may each be regarded as varieties of ownership. The rights to use, income, or possession standing alone, are perhaps disputable cases, but seem to me to be too slender to support the claim of ownership. When each is buttressed with some version of absence of term or the right to security, the claim of ownership is plausible. I think it is safe to say that any subset which could reasonably be called a variety of ownership would have to include at least one of the first five elements (possession, use, management, income, capital).

These, then, are the likely candidates for varieties of ownership. The right to capital alone; and thus capital plus any other element or set of elements. The right to security in possession, or in use, or in income, or in management; thus each of these pairs plus any other element or set of elements. The number of combinations (about 1500 out of a total of 2047 possible for the eleven elements) is daunting. When varying definitions and scopes are added for each element, the number is greatly increased.

Needless to say, the analysis to follow will not be able to concern itself explicitly with very many of these combinations. (And one suspects that most of the variants of the main types listed above are not significantly different, for philosophical purposes, from those which will be considered.) But a lively appreciation of the range possible for property rights will be central to the discussion.

PROPERTY RIGHTS AND THE GENERAL NATURE OF THE RIGHTS-RELATIONSHIP

A further point which must be kept in mind — and which Honoré's analysis shows nicely — is that property rights are typically aggregates of different sorts of rights and rights-correlatives. The right to possess is to be sharply distinguished from mere protection of possession once achieved — that is, it is a claim right to have possession, not merely a power to acquire or a liberty to keep. If I have the right to possess a thing, others do not merely have 'no right' that I not possess it; they have a duty not to interfere with my possession — perhaps even to see to it that the thing is restored to me if lost.

The right to use is primarily a liberty reinforced with claim rights excluding others from interference. But note that it is interference with use, not possession, which is excluded. The two may sometimes come to the same thing, but particularly in the case of land, they often do not.

The right to manage is part liberty, part power, again reinforced with exclusionary claim rights. The right to income is part liberty and part power, and the right to the capital is the same. Both are typically buttressed with claim rights.

Security, defined with the term 'immunity,' is just that, as is absence of term. They are rights which correlate with disabilities in others.

Transmissibility is a power. It might be thought that the right to alienate (i.e. transfer by exchange or gift, or simply give up to no one in particular) includes this, but since bequests are only gifts post mortem as it were, they are best considered separately from the right to alienate.

The prohibition of harmful use is a duty. Liability to execution for debt is a Hohfeldian liability. And residuary character is a compound of liabilities, no rights, duties, and their correlatives.

SUMMARY OF CAUTIONARY REMARKS ON PROPERTY RIGHTS
First, though the term 'property rights' is not unequivocal either in legal or moral contexts, it seems best to understand it as referring to one's proprietary rights (as opposed to personal rights) in general — that is, to all proprietary rights, whether *in rem, in personam,* over either corporeal, or incorporeal things. Second, such proprietary rights are the rights of ownership, and those rights are complex. None of the characteristics which define the full or liberal notion of ownership in modern legal systems is necessary to all varieties of ownership. And each characteristic is subject to variations in definition and scope. The result is that there are a wide variety of sets of rights which, when they are held by someone, can justify the claim that that person owns something. A philosophical discussion will have to pay close attention to the nature of any particular aggregate of ownership rights which may be at issue. Third, one will need to pay attention to the fact that the rights at stake may be of different (Hohfeldian) sorts; to the fact that restrictions on the scope of various rights (or changes in their definitions) may be crucial with respect to whether they can be justified; and to the fact that different aggregates of ownership rights for different things may be justified by the same line of argument (e.g. utility may not justify capital rights in land but have no trouble with capital rights in other things). All this seems obvious, but even a cursory look at the history of the discussion of property rights will show how frequently such distinctions have been ignored or misused.

Justification
The justification of a property right will mean, in what follows, its assertion as a conclusion from a sound, 'all things considered,' reasoned argument. People can, of course, have unjustified and/or unjustifiable legal and moral rights, *de facto,* by virtue of a prevailing legal or moral code. Whether such *de facto* rights are 'real' or not I leave to one side as a question without significant philosophical interest. To the other side I leave questions as to whether there are any rights people ought to have which, while they cannot be justified, are none the less known to be just by intuition, revelation, or the 'moral sense.' Intuition and revelation are good places to begin a philosophical discussion, but they are bad places to end it. When I speak of a right people *have*, then, I shall rely on the context to make clear whether I mean a *de facto* right or one which can be justified as a conclusion from a sound, all things

considered, reasoned argument.

By an 'all things considered' argument, I mean one which does not restrict itself to a special subset of reasons — reasons of legality, utility, prudence, etiquette, or reasons drawn from a special conception of morality which excludes all reference to utility and prudence. An 'all things considered' argument is one which includes any consideration relevant to a given conclusion, and in fact, unless some reason is given to the contrary, gives considerations of each sort equal weight. I have argued elsewhere that this sort of inclusive justification is properly called *moral* justification;[15] but regardless of the soundness of that argument, it is certainly the sort of justification the moral philosopher must eventually make. Everything else is preliminary.

A final word about justification: I shall distinguish, throughout what follows, three levels of justification. A *general* justification of property rights gives an answer to the question of why there ought to be any property rights — of any sort — at all. A *specific* justification gives an answer to the question of why there ought to be a specific *sort* of property right (e.g. full, liberal ownership of land). A *particular* justification gives an answer to the question of why a particular person ought to have a particular property right in a particular thing.

With these preliminaries out of the way, then, I shall turn to the main task — the analysis of traditional arguments for and against private property. (Again I shall often drop the modifier 'private' and speak only of property rights or the rights of ownership. The context will make it quite clear whether the modifier 'private' is implicit or not.)

3 The Argument from First Occupancy

When the question arises as to why some people, rather than others, should own things, one of the issues which comes to mind is the question, 'Who had it first?' The notion that being there first somehow justifies ownership rights is a venerable and persistent one. A close analysis will show that it does not provide a sound basis for claims to ownership, and thus contributes nothing to a theory of the general justification of property rights. But it is important to consider none the less. The reasons for its failure are illuminating.

A priori restrictions on first occupancy claims

There are times when 'I was here first' *seems* to make some sense as a rationale for the claim 'It's mine,' but those times are special in character, and the limitations on the property claims which can plausibly be made are severe. First occupancy obviously cannot justify title to property unless (1) the object occupied is unowned; *and* (2) occupation is in some relevant sense actual as opposed to intentional or declaratory; *and* (3) the concept of actual occupation defines with reasonable clarity how much one can occupy; *and* (4) the occupier claims no more than a share as defined by (3). The first requirement comes simply from the fact that if the thing is already owned by someone, mere occupation will not change that fact, and presumably *first* occupation is by definition impossible. The second requirement (as will be shown) is necessary to avoid making the concept of occupation altogether absurd and self-defeating. The third and fourth requirements arise, not because one needs, in justice, to put a limit on what a person can rightfully appropriate in this way (though that may also be true), but because one has to be able to specify how much an occupier occupies in order to make sense of the notion of occupation to begin with, and once such limits are specified, they define the maximum an occupier could ever rightfully claim merely on the basis of occupation. Whether an occupier *can* rightfully claim this maximum — or indeed any amount at all — is a separate issue. I shall discuss each of the four requirements first, and then turn to the question of the soundness of the argument.

THE THING OCCUPIED MUST BELONG TO NO ONE

First occupancy is put forward as a mode of 'original' acquisition. As such it cannot operate where the thing occupied is already owned. But what about things which are not owned by anyone? Property theorists have typically said that such things are common property, or belong to everyone in common, and as such can (or cannot) be appropriated by individuals. Cicero invites readers to think of unappropriated things as seats in a public theater where one can take whatever seat is vacant (but no more than one).[1] Others have not been convinced by the metaphor.

A distinction of some importance for this issue was urged by Pufendorf, and is incorporated in the first requirement stated here. Pufendorf sharply distinguished cases in which things were held in common 'positively' — that is, were jointly owned, everyone having a well-defined share — and cases in which things were held in common only 'negatively' — that is, were owned by no one but were equally available to everyone.[2] The importance of the distinction for the theory of first occupancy may be made clear in the following way.

Where a thing is jointly owned and one's share is therefore well defined, there is no room for first occupancy claims. It is clear that first occupancy can never create a justifiable title independent of the consent of the joint owners. When a thing is jointly owned in the full liberal sense, for example, any disposition of the thing by one person without the consent of the others is a violation of their rights of ownership — even if one has taken no more than one's share. Joint ownership means joint management, and more fundamentally, joint right to the capital. And though there may be cases in which adherence to the first occupier rule (among the joint owners) is the only rational method for allocating specific shares among the owners, still the decision to allocate specific shares at all must be a joint decision. Indeed, there is a decision of considerable import to be made in defining what ownership rights will be allocated, even if an allocation has been decided on. Will the group give up joint ownership altogether? Or merely possessory and use rights? If use rights, then rights to income as well? And so forth.

Where a thing is owned by no one, however, no objections to appropriation can come from a previous title, and the defender of first occupancy merely has to show how taking possession of something creates any of the rights of property. This has turned out to be difficult, as I shall show below.

OCCUPATION MUST BE, IN SOME RELEVANT SENSE, ACTUAL AS OPPOSED TO MERELY INTENTIONAL OR DECLARATORY

This second requirement, as I noted earlier, is necessary to avoid making the concept of occupation altogether absurd and self-defeating. After all, if a mere foothold on a continent is enough to establish first occupancy of all the uninhabited regions of the continent, then a foothold in the universe is enough to claim first occupancy of the uninhabited regions of the whole cosmos. As Rousseau remarks, after satirizing the 'appropriations' of European explorers, 'On such a showing. . . the Catholic King need only take possession, from his apartment, of the whole universe, merely making a subsequent reservation about what was already in the possession of [others].'[3] So occupation must be 'actual,' but what does that mean?

It means, first of all, that mere intentions or declarations do not count. First occupancy is supposed to be a mode of original acquisition, independent of conventions. While, under the strictures of well-defined conventions, it might be reasonable to allow certain people to 'occupy' by declaration (as in telephoning an airline reservation), or by token (as in buying a ticket for a concert), in the absence of such conventions these acts cannot count as occupancy without reducing the whole procedure to the self-defeating absurdity noted above. So occupation must involve the actual physical presence of the occupier (or perhaps a proxy). But how much territory does one's presence 'occupy'? Only the area equal to one's physical size? In most cases such a rule would be as absurd as allowing occupation by declaration. But if the area said to be occupied is not limited to one's physical size, then how is it to be limited? That it *must* be limited is clear (we all have footholds in the universe . . .). So a rationale for a principle of limitation must be found if the notion of appropriation by occupation is to make sense of all.

A reasonable position — and, I think, partly what lies behind the classic requirement that one occupy no more than one can use — is that the amount one can be said to appropriate with one's presence be determined by one's purpose in occupying the thing and one's carrying out of that purpose *at the time of occupation*. The rationale for such a requirement is as follows.

Occupation, while it must be a physical presence in or on the thing, cannot be only that if it is to count as an appropriation. It must also be for the *purpose* of appropriation; otherwise, there would be no difference between the state of merely *being* somewhere and the act of appropriating that place. One may appropriate things for various purposes: to have a place to live, to hunt, to cultivate, to mine, or perhaps just to keep to oneself. If a person takes a piece of land to cultivate, but does not carry out his purpose, his appropriation of anything more than the area on which he stands is purely intentional. The cultivated land, however, is reasonably regarded as occupied by the cultivator (even though he may be physically present on only part of it), and the cultivation effectively defines the limits of the land so appropriated. Similarly for other purposes of appropriation: if one's purpose is simply to exclude others, then until one effectively does so (i.e. has the will and the ability to do so) one's appropriation is purely intentional. The declarations of European explorers in the fifteenth century were mostly of this purely intentional sort, as would be that of a United States astronaut were he to try to appropriate the moon. No effective means of excluding others from a whole continent existed in the case of Cortez or Coronado, and none exists now in the case of the moon. Should it ever be otherwise, however — as for example it would be if the science fiction idea of impenetrable planetary defenses were realized — then we could make sense of the notion that a nation or a person could appropriate a planet by occupation, merely for the purpose of excluding others. (This would not, by itself, *justify* property rights in the whole planet, of course. But the concept of *occupation* of the whole planet, in a sense requisite for appropriation, would clearly be satisfied.) A rancher with a herd of three cattle, then, cannot occupy, in the sense requisite for appropriation of pasture land, a 5,000 acre tract. He could, however, appropriate acreage for future use (i.e. to exclude others until his herd grows) to the extent that he could actually keep others off the land.

It might be thought that the wide variety of purposes possible for appropriations makes the foregoing account as liable to absurdity as one which admits simple declarations. Suppose I appropriate merely for self-aggrandizement, and having an exalted view of myself, decide that only a continent would be sufficient to make me grander than I am? Or suppose I appropriate a mountain range for aesthetic purposes? Or 5,000 acres for privacy? Doesn't the existence of such purposes entail, in effect, appropriation by mere intent? I think not. Such 'interior' purposes either require the exclusion of others for their implementation, and thus are limited in the same way that appropriations purely for the exclusion of others are limited, or else they do not require occupation at all (as when I make a song 'my own'). In that case they can be accomplished by intent or declaration alone, and have only

27

that status. All of the potentially embarrassing cases I can think of fall into one or the other of these categories. The quantitative limits of appropriation by occupation, then, in the senses relevant to a discussion of property rights, are reasonably regarded as the limits of the purposes of such appropriations *as implemented.*

OCCUPATION MUST BE ACTUAL AND NO MORE THAN ONE'S SHARE
The concept of actual occupation, as explicated above, now defines with reasonable clarity how much one can occupy, so the third requirement is met. And since it requires physical presence at least of a sort necessary to implement the purpose for which appropriation by occupation is undertaken, one is limited, by definition, to the share so defined. Thus the requirement that the occupier may claim (to have occupied) no more than a' share as so defined is satisfied. The question now is simply whether first occupancy, even under these stringent conditions, can ever legitimate a claim of propery rights.

Arguments for first occupancy

To begin, it should be pointed out again that possession — even possession protected by social agreement or law — is to be sharply distinguished from the claim right to possess. If one has a claim right to possess a certain seat in a theatre, then others have a duty either to turn it over on demand or to forbear altogether from possessing it themselves. But your possession of an unreserved seat may be protected (as the legitimate exercise of a liberty), as long as you occupy it, without any recognition of a claim right to possession, or any of the other rights of ownership. It is proof of the existence of a claim right to possess, derived from the fact of first occupancy, with which one must be concerned. And that is a very difficult task.

There are, as far as I can tell, only five lines of argument which have ever purported to do it. Two are flatly defective; a third is reducible to the labor theory of acquisition; the fourth is a version of the argument from utility; and the fifth, while more promising, is so general in form that the reference to first occupation is eliminable.

KANT'S REMARKS
The first of the two defective lines is an argument attributed to Kant.[4] He argued that an act of will in appropriating a thing creates a property right in that thing if the act satisfies the moral law and if anyone else's subsequent use or possession of it would injure the appropriator. On the assumption that at least some acts of first occupancy can satisfy the moral law (i.e. are capable of being derived from a self-consistent

universal law), Kant claims (1) that to deny anyone the exercise of freedom involved in such an appropriation would be wrong, and (2) that once appropriated, to deny anyone the continued use of the possession would be wrong. These things would be wrong in so far as they would be unjustifiable restrictions of the exercise of a person's freedom. Let us see what follows from this and what is assumed by it.

If (as Kant evidently thinks) I have a natural right to, or it would in some other sense be wrong to deny me, the greatest extent of liberty compatible with the moral law, then it would follow that the denial of the exercise of my freedom to appropriate (in accord with the moral law) would be wrong. But it does not follow at all from the fact that *appropriation* conforms to the moral law that *permanent possession,* use, management, right to income, capital, and power of transmission *also* conform to the moral law. No doubt expropriation would 'injure' me in the sense that it would frustrate the exercise of my freedom. But if expropriation is ever consistent with the moral law, and indeed with the greatest extent of liberty compatible with the moral law, then the 'injury' to me would not be a wrong. There is no reason to think, *a priori,* that this could not sometimes be the case. In short, the argument establishes a liberty right to appropriate but not a claim right to keep. And that is not a property right at all. (An extension of the argument from natural liberty *can* support the justification of property rights — in a way which connects indirectly with first occupation — but that is best left to later discussion. See below, pp. 75-80.)

HEGEL'S REMARKS

The second defective line is attributable to Hegel. At least it is suggested by passages from his *Philosophy of Right*.[5] There, mixed together with some interesting remarks about the genesis of property as an expression of personality, Hegel asserts that (1) 'a person must translate his freedom into an external sphere to exist as Idea'; (2) what is external is what is not personal, not free, without rights; and (3) 'a person has as his substantive end the right of putting his will into any and every [external] thing'; (4) this putting of the will into a thing makes it one's own 'because it has no such end in itself and derives its destiny and soul from his will'; (5) this is, he concludes, 'the absolute right of appropriation which man has over all things.'

The criticism of the argument may be brief. I do not grant that the need asserted in (1) must include the acquisition of property rights. Nor do I grant, as a general principle, that a need creates a property right; therefore I am suspicious of the move from (1) to (3). But clearly the argument, even granting (1), (2), and (3), has the same flaw as

Kant's. It proves at most a right to appropriate but not to keep. It cannot follow simply from the fact that I have a right to put my will into something (i.e. appropriate it) that I have the right to indefinite possession and capital, for example. So again, an argument for first occupation has not proved a property right.

LABOR, UTILITY, AND 'WHY NOT?' ARGUMENTS[6]

The other lines of argument may be dealt with just as summarily. The third is that by virtue of the labor which I invest in a thing by occupying it, given certain other conditions, I come to own it. This is clearly a version of the labor theory as much as it is a version of first occupancy, and is better dealt with below. The fourth is an argument from utility: it is a fact of nature, this one goes, that a socially unstable situation will result if people are not allowed to keep (in some sense of ownership) what they first occupy. But this surely contains a very dubious premise about human psychology, and must depend, as well, on a very contestable view of how ruthlessly a government can act while still preserving order. We have ample evidence that gross acts of expropriation can be 'smoothed over' by ruthless suppression of dissent. In any case, utility arguments will be considered in more detail below.

Finally, there is what might be called the 'why not?' argument. In the absence of prior rights, the argument goes, and since the fellow has gone to the trouble to take it (and would doubtless welcome property rights if not actively resent the withholding of them), and if there are no good reasons to the contrary, why not grant the rights? That is, it would not be unjustifiable to grant them. I will have more to say about this argument later, but suffice it now to note that the reference to occupation is either eliminable (after all, if there are no good reasons against it, and anyone whoever − occupier or not − wants property rights, then why not?) or else it is really a reference to the labor involved in occupation, and the argument becomes a version of the labor theory.

Conclusion

The argument from first occupation, then, does not succeed in giving a general justification of property rights. That is, it provides no answer to the question of why there ought to be any property rights (based on first occupancy) at all. Liberty to occupy (under certain conditions), yes. But not any of the complexes of claim rights, liberties, powers, or immunities comprising something which could reasonably be described as ownership.

However, if another general justification can be found, and if (for some reason — reasons of utility, perhaps) it is settled that first occupancy ought to be recognized as a way for particular individuals to obtain property rights, then the notion would have some interesting results for the specific justification of these rights.[7] For example, occupation by cultivation limits what is occupied to what is cultivated. If it is right (for other reasons) to confer ownership rights on the cultivator, those rights would presumably be limited to those required for cultivation. The farmer would thus have no right to exclude picnickers from a fallow field, or bathers from a pond, as long as they did not interfere with the cultivation. This principle of innocent use is quite a general one: owners have only those rights required for the purposes of their occupation.

As for particular justification — that is, the determination of who owns what — occupation provides a clear criterion *once the correctness of using the first occupancy principle has been established.* The most convincing discussions of first occupancy are precisely of this sort — attempts to show that *since we grant that things should be owned by someone,* a good place for the law (or morality) to begin to sort out titles is with the first (ascertainable) appropriation of a given thing. One then examines (legal or moral) objections to the original appropriation and to subsequent transfers. But this is not a part of any *general* justification of property. It assumes the general justifiability of the institution and deals rather with questions of particular justification.

4 The Labor Theory of Property Acquisition

The root idea

The root idea of the labor theory is that people are entitled to hold, as property, whatever they produce by their own initiative, intelligence, and industry. It is an idea which, once enunciated in the context of natural rights theories of the seventeenth century, has seemed nearly inescapable and self-evident. Yet it is worth remembering that it only emerges 'naturally' from a very particular theoretical context — specifically, the attempt to build up an account of the just society from an (imaginary) state of nature in which there were no rules, no obligations, no political relations of superior to inferior, and in which all things were held in common. Outside the confines of state-of-nature theory (as, for example, in ancient Greek political theory), the right to the product of one's labor is hardly mentioned at all, and never made a cornerstone of the theory of property. Indeed, it is barely mentioned even in state-of-nature theorists as late as Grotius and Pufendorf.[1] But once the idea had clearly emerged, it became virtually unchallengeable. One might ignore it (as Hume did), but would not deny it, even if one were attacking the whole notion of 'primitive acquisition.'[2]

Oddly, proponents of the labor theory rarely discuss the warrant for its root idea. That is, they rarely argue for it as a general justification of property rights. (It is, of course, *used* as a general justification, but that is quite another matter.) There are intricate arguments about the *specific sorts* of property rights labor can produce (whether it can give title to land, or only to produce from land, and whether it can yield the right of transmission, for example). But there is scant evidence, outside of Locke, of any serious thinking about how it is that labor can entitle anyone to anything. Time and again writers profess their inability to think of any alternative to it (short of a social compact) which could produce property rights. But the absence of a valid alternative proves nothing about the validity of the case at hand, and previous 'alternatives' (such as one of the strands which runs through Christian property theory to the effect that the land belongs to the righteous, or what presumably would have been Aristotle's view, that property ought to be held by people who can use it properly) are not considered. Locke, however, made the effort, and so I shall organize my account (loosely) around his arguments.

Locke's theory

There are several distinct arguments in Locke[3] for a labor theory of primitive acquisition, and they involve two distinct conceptions of the root idea that labor entitles one to property. The standardly quoted line is this:

(1a) Everyone 'has a property in his own person; this nobody has a right to but himself.' (27)

(1b) '[T] he labour of his body and the work of his hands we may say are properly his.' (27)

(1c) Whenever someone, by his labor, changes a thing from its natural state (to make it more useful or beneficial to him [26, 28, 34]), he has 'mixed' his labor with it — that is, 'joined to it something that is his own.' (27)

(1d) He 'thereby makes it his property,' for 'it hath, by this labour, something annexed to it that excludes the common right of other men. For this labour being the unquestionable property of the labourer, no man but he can have a right to what that is once joined to. . . . ' (27)

(1e) This is so 'at least where there is enough and as good left in common for others' (27), and where what one takes is no more than one can use. (31)

The root idea is here understood in terms of a derivation from prior property rights. Since one's body is one's property, and its produce (labor) is also one's property, it follows (?) that the labor's product is also one's property. Critics have generally focused on the final inference rather than the premises behind it, and they have had good sport with the metaphors of 'mixing,' 'annexing,' or 'joining' one's labor to a thing.

But these metaphors really pose no more difficult a problem than is posed by the need to define the extent of one's 'occupation' of a piece of land; both problems can be solved in much the same way. Labor is first distinguished from mere intent, declaration, or occupation. It is next distinguished from play and accidental improvement (e.g. playfully pushing a boulder into a boulder field and accidentaly starting an avalanche which clears the field and makes it suitable pasture for

33

sheep).[4] One then simply calls attention to the fact that labor is purposive. Some efforts are for the purpose of enclosing a piece of land; some are for growing a crop; others are for creating an artifact to be possessed and used. The extent of the land (or whatever) with which one's labor 'mixes' is thus quite naturally defined by the purposes for which one labors. Erecting a fence counts as a mixing of labor with the enclosed area, and cultivation counts as laboring on the soil. There are puzzling cases, embarrassing cases (what about the airspace over the land?). But on the whole, the metaphors are manageable ones.

The crucial problem with premises (c) and (d) is, as Nozick puts it, why anyone should think that mixing one's labor with a thing is a way of making the thing one's own rather than a way of losing one's labor.[5] It is evident that Locke was not content with these premises either. He keeps adding remarks which produce variants of the original argument. For example, consider this variant:

(2a) People have property in their bodies (as in argument 1).

(2b) Likewise, their labor is their property (as in argument 1).

(2c) 'That labour put[s] a distinction between [the thing worked on] and [what is held in] common.' (28)

(2d) The distinction is that labor 'added something to [the thing] more than nature . . . had done. . . . ' (28)

(2e) The thing labor adds — the difference it makes — is value. Things that are unappropriated are 'of no use' (28) and labor is responsible for nine-tenths or perhaps ninety-nine hundredths of the value of the products of the earth. (40)

(2f) Therefore one's labor entitles one to property in the thing labored on.

Strictly, of course, the argument could at most only yield the conclusion that one is entitled to the value one's labor adds to the thing, and not to the thing itself. Locke's reply would apparently have been that the difference is minuscule (some 1 per cent) and that in some cases the labor value and the thing so improved are inseparable. Nineteenth-century critics — anarchists, socialists, and reform capitalists alike — insist quite correctly, however, that the argument does not support property in land.[6] In the products of labor, yes. But in the case of land those are the fruits of cultivation, or herding, or building, and not the land itself. The difference here is not a small one and the two are not inseparable.

But is the argument sound? It apparently proceeds by assuming that the property in one's body 'extends' first to (the body's product) labor, and then again to the product of labor *by the alteration in one's relation to the thing which is the consequence of the labor.* But how is this so? Granted that when one labors on a thing, one's relation to it has been changed – i.e. before the laboring, the thing could not truly be described as something one had labored on; after the laboring, it can be so described. But how does that change justify the claim that one has property rights in the thing?

I shall comment on this argument in detail in a moment, but first let me lay out the final variant of the labor theory which can be found in Locke. This one, though it is less often quoted, is the heart of the issue as I see it. It begins by repeating premises (2a) through (2e):

(3a) People have property in their bodies (as in arguments 1, 2).

(3b) Likewise, their labor is their property (as in arguments 1, 2).

(3c) 'That labour put [s] a distinction between [the thing worked on] and [what is held in] common.' (28)

(3d) The distinction is that labor 'added something to [the thing] more than nature . . . had done. . . . .' (28)

(3e) The thing labor adds – the difference it makes – is value. Things that are unappropriated are 'of no use' (28) and labor is responsible for nine-tenths or perhaps ninety-nine hundredths of the value of the products of the earth. (40)

Then the new argument adds the following:

(3f) Since things are of no use until appropriated (28), and appropriation in most cases involves labor which would not be undertaken except for the expected benefits, to let others have the 'benefits of another's pains' (34) would clearly be unjust.

(3g) This is so 'at least where there is enough and as good left in common for others' (27) and where one takes no more than one can use (31). 'For he that leaves as much as another can make use of, does as good as take nothing at all.'

(3h) Therefore, from (a) through (e) one is entitled to the whole of the value one's labor adds to things, and from (f) and (g) – together with elements from (a) through (e) – one is entitled to the other expected benefits as well.

Here, in (3f) and (3g), is a variant of the root idea quite distinct from that expressed in (a) through (e). The proposal is that labor is something unpleasant enough so that people only do it in the expectation of benefits (and since unlabored-on things are of little or no value anyway), it would be unjust not to let people have the benefits they take pains to get. This is so at least where one's appropriation has no significant effect on others.

Here (3g) – premise (1e) in the original argument – functions as much to disarm objections as to state a positive requirement of justice. Premises (f) and (g), then, taken together, constitute an argument for the benefits people expect, but cannot get title to from premises (a) through (e). If these benefits are ones people deserve by virtue of the (labor) pains they have taken, then that constitutes a good reason for granting the benefits. And if there are no countervailingly strong reasons to the contrary, granting them is justified. This explication of the root idea has seldom been attacked.

Locke gives, then, two distinct reasons for thinking that one's labor entitles one to property in the thing labored on: (1) that such rights derive from prior property rights in one's body and its labors; and (2) that such rights are required, in justice, as a return for the laborer's pains. Both reasons, taken together, are intended to establish security in the right to capital and the other rights normally associated with capital — namely, possessory, use, management, and income rights. Absence of term is also supposed to follow, and the prohibition of harmful use (probably) follows from the restrictions in (3g). Liability to execution for debt may perhaps be ground out of an analysis of the powers of alienation (promises governing exchanges). At least it is consistent with a rational system of exchanges. Transmissibility, however, does not follow directly from Locke's arguments, as has been noted by some.[7]

Criticism of Locke's theory

Critics of these arguments have not carefully distinguished them, and have often contented themselves with attacks on the 'mixing' metaphors in the first argument and the self-defeating character of the labor theory as applied to ownership of land (the fact that, once all the land is owned by a proper subset of the population, the landless, while they must work on the land, are denied the whole fruits of their labors by the results of the very arguments which were supposed to guarantee them).

Proudhon goes farther than this in two directions: by calling attention to what he takes to be an ambiguity in premises (3a) and (3b), and by scoffing at the 'taking pains' part of (3f). Clearly, these are crucial lines of attack, for they go to the heart of each of the two interpretations of the labor theory's root idea. Neither line of attack has gotten the development it needs. I intend to remedy that in what follows, beginning in each case from Proudhon's sketchy remarks.

PROPERTY RIGHTS IN ONE'S BODY[8]

Some people have thought that premise (a) involves Locke's argument in an equivocal use of the term 'property.' Proudhon says: 'The word property has two meanings: 1. It designates the quality which makes a thing what it is . . . 2. It expresses the right of absolute control over a thing. . . . To tell a poor man that he HAS property because he *HAS* arms and legs . . . is to play upon words, and to add insult to injury.'[9] As Black's law dictionary points out, older writers sometimes used the word in the sense of 'that which is proper to someone,' and Salmond[10] cites Locke as among those who use it to refer to 'all that is [one's] in law.'

It is conceivable that Locke equivocated in his use of 'property.' But it is unlikely that Locke equivocated *in this passage;* and it is certain that the argument in no way *depends* on equivocation. (Nor does it depend on the concept of a mysterious soul-substance which 'owns' its body.) Property rights in one's body can be perfectly well understood merely as the correlatives of other people's duties to forbear from acting so as to possess, use, and manage one's body. Property rights here, as in the standard cases of ownership, are fundamentally rights to *exclude* others. As such, assertions that my body is my property are not logically troublesome.

Locke says nothing about where these property rights come from, but I suspect it is wisest to regard them as simply summations of the relevant aspects of one's rights to life and liberty. Even so, a close look at the relations between these rights and the rights to the produce of one's labor produces some surprising results.

The fact is that without some modification of one or both propositions, 'Everyone has property in his own body' and 'Everyone is entitled to the fruit of his labors' are strictly incompatible. They are incompatible because, supposing both are true of everyone, then either (1) parents are entitled to property rights in their children (as the fruit of their labor), in which case not all people have property rights in their own bodies (namely, those with living parents who have not relinquished their rights in their children, or those whose parents have assigned the rights to others who are living and have not relinquished them); or (2) parents are not entitled to property rights in their children, in which case they are not (always) entitled to property rights in the fruits of their labor.

Whichever one of these alternatives is considered sound, Locke's argument must be revised to avoid the contradiction. If children do not have property rights in their bodies, the necessary revisions produce a picture of human relationships repugnant to modern readers. (Though it is notable that this is, in part, purely a modern phenomenon. Writers as late as Grotius, for example, record without objection the recognition of parental property rights in children by some societies.[11]) Specifically, people would start life quite literally as their parents' chattels, and so continue until freed by manumission, default, or emancipation. It is clear that Locke would have accepted no such revision of the premises, if for no other reason than that it would eliminate property as a natural right except for the small class of people whose parents die intestate. Further, of course, there is no way to make the consequences of such revisions compatible with natural rights accounts of liberty and equality.

Repugnance to modern sensibilities is not, by itself, an argument against this revision of Locke's premises, of course. And there is certainly enough dispute about the validity of natural rights theory to mean that the revision cannot simply be dismissed by pointing out its incompatibility with the requirements of that theory. But the wholesale nature of the changes which would result from the adoption of the revised premises − changes which would conflict with fundamental principles held even on utilitarian grounds − suggest that there would have to be better reasons than merely the preservation of one of Locke's arguments for property rights to justify adoption of the revised premises.

But suppose instead of insisting that not everyone has rights to their bodies, one takes the other alternative and insists that people do not always have a right to the products of their labors? Specifically, that they do not have such rights when their labor produces other people. Very well. But how is such a restriction to be justified as anything other than an *ad hoc* device to square Locke's argument with conventional moral principles? There seem again to be two possibilities: (1) that there is something in the nature of labor which justifies a property claim for some products but not for others; or (2) that the labor claim is valid in all cases, just overridden in some by conflicting claims.

I know of no way to take the first possibility. It is true that writers have often spoken of some things as not acquirable by occupation or labor (the sea, the air). But these arguments are usually unsound (as when Grotius speaks of the sea as unbounded and therefore unoccupiable[12]). The air and the sea *can* be appropriated by labor − bottled and compressed in the one case, drained off in the other. In any event, if anything is clearly a product of (one's body's) labor, a child is. It seems unlikely that anything will be found in the nature of the *labor* involved in conception, gestation, birth, and nurturing which will distinguish it sufficiently from the labor involved in cultivating a garden to justify using the latter in a Lockean argument but forbidding the use of the former.

The second possibility − the conflicting claims alternative − is surely the obvious line. One asserts first that persons have rights other than those to the fruits of their labor. This means others have duties corresponding to those rights. Such duties – e.g. my parents' duty to respect my liberty – may conflict with their property rights in me. Where a duty conflicts with a right it may (a) be overridden by the right; (b) be equal to and therefore effectively 'cancel' the right; or (c) override the right. The question now to be answered is why the duty of parents to respect the liberty of their children either cancels or overrides their property rights in those children.

The long answer would have to go through the whole account of rights to life and liberty, showing their dominance over property rights. But fortunately there is a shorter argument available in this case. Locke makes the right to property in the fruits of one's labor *derivative* from one's rights to one's body (at least he does so in the standardly quoted line of argument). If the property rights in one's body are merely summations of – or another way of stating – the rights to liberty all humans are entitled to, then it is clear that we have grounds for restricting the consequences of a principle derived from those rights (namely, the principle that people are entitled to property in the fruits of their labor) to results which are compatible with the 'originating' rights (namely, the liberty rights). That is, we can rule out as self-contradictory any consequence of a principle which contradicts the premises which generate that principle. If we begin from the premise that all people have property rights in their bodies, and from that generate the principle that they are entitled to the produce of their labors, we cannot accept an interpretation of that principle which permits a property right in the produce of labor to outweigh or cancel a person's property right in his or her body. For the latter sort of right is primary; it is *from* that that property rights to labor's produce derive.

This also solves nicely the problem of accounting for the *existence* of property rights in one's body. After all, in Locke's account, labor is supposed to be the only mode of original or primitive acquisition, and if anyone acquires property in people's bodies that way it is parents, not the people themselves. So where do these 'prior' property rights come from? Thinking of them as restatements of rights to life and liberty gives a good answer. Of course it also means that property rights – in this one argument at least – *derive* from rights to life and liberty, and therefore one's success in establishing property rights by that argument depends on success in establishing those other rights. But this is a consequence natural rights theorists would accept gladly, I think.

The failure of the 'property rights in one's body' line of argument. What they might not accept as gladly is the way the account just given makes painfully clear the need to further restrict the property rights so derived. If their source in people's liberty means that persons cannot be owned, does it not also mean that ownership of land must be restricted? 'Place one hundred men on an island from which there is no escape, and whether you make one of these men the absolute owner of the other ninety-nine or the absolute owner of the soil of the island, will make no difference either to him or to them.'[13] Where ownership of anything (land, water, etc.) has the effect of abridging the liberty (property in one's body) from which the Lockean argument derives the rights of ownership over things other than one's body, the argument cannot permit such ownership.

Worse still, the basic question remains unsettled: How is it that the property rights to one's body 'transfer' or extend to property in the products of one's labor? In so far as one's labor is inseparable (by way of ownership rights) from one's body, it is understandable how the first 'extension' — from ownership of the body to ownership of the labor — is warranted. But the same can hardly be said for the second extension — from ownership of the labor to ownership of labor's products. The products of one's labors are clearly separable from one's body. And Nozick's question remains: Why is it that investing one's labor in something causes one to come to own that thing? Why does it not instead just mean that one has lost the investment?

Here defenders of the labor theory tend to make a burden-of-proof argument. Why not? they say. Surely my working on something *changes* things. I now stand in a relation to the thing labored on which differentiates me from all other persons. I produced its human value (or nine-tenths or ninety-nine hundredths of it). Surely that makes it *mine*.

Unfortunately, this will not work. The phrase 'It is mine' is ambiguous here. As a reference to the fact that it (the produce of one's labor) *is* just that — and not the produce of anyone else's, or a product of chance — the claim 'It is mine' is of course true, but merely a repetition of the assertion of the unique relation which now holds between you and the thing. The crucial question remains unanswered: What reason is there to conclude that this altered relationship constitutes, or warrants, or gives any support at all to the claim that you have ownership rights in the thing? Why does it not just mean that you are entitled to public admiration? Or the gratitude of your fellows? Or perhaps nothing more than the appropriate change in the great book which describes the world? It is labor theorists who are making the assertion here — that the changes produced by their labors entitle them to property rights. The burden of proof is on them to show how it is so, and they have not done so. I see no reason to think that they can. I suspect that what they *can* show is the reasonability (in some cases) of saying that labor grounds a *recipient claim right* to the thing. That is, that the fact of one's labor can sometimes establish that one is owed possession or use or management in the sense that, should one not get it, one could appropriately react as though an *unspecifiable* duty-bearer had violated one's claim rights. But that is not a property right, and so whether or not the labor theory establishes it is irrelevant here.

ENTITLEMENT TO THE PRODUCTS OF ONE'S LABOR

But isn't one *entitled* to those products none the less? Most people since Locke have said, assumed, or implied an affirmative answer, and shifted to the other major argument from labor to do it. Locke puts it in the form of an entitlement for one's 'pains' in creating something valuable out of raw and largely useless material. I took the *trouble* to make it; I deserve some reward for my efforts; I *earned* it by my efforts. The sentiment is a familiar and powerful one. But to see just how little it proves – at least in the way Locke uses it – consider this exchange between Proudhon and Mill.

Proudhon scoffs at the whole idea, quoting someone else: 'The rich have the arrogance to say. "I built this wall, I earned this land with my labor." Who set you the tasks? we may reply, and by what right do you demand payment from us for labor which we did not impose on you?' Proudhon says, 'All sophistry falls to the ground in the presence of this argument.'[14] Mill salvages the 'sophistry,' in a passage specifically *not* referring to property in *land,* in the following way: 'It is no hardship to anyone, to be excluded from what others have produced: [the producers] were not bound to produce it for his use, and he loses nothing by not sharing in what otherwise would not have existed at all.'[15]

Mill has gotten, I think, as close as one can get to an account of how Locke's 'taking pains' argument justifies a property claim: when the labor is (1) beyond what is required, morally, that one do for others; (2) produces something which would not have existed except for it; and (3) its product is something which others lose nothing by being excluded from; then (4) it is not wrong for producers to exclude others from the possession, use, etc. of the fruits of their labors. It is not so much that the producers *deserve* the produce of their labors. It is rather that no one else does, and it is not wrong for the laborer to have them. Then, in so far as instituting a system of property rights which guarantees to laborers the fruits of their labor is a justifiable way of excluding others (as under the three conditions above), such property rights are justifiable.

The prior demands of morality. Notice, however, the severe restrictions on what this argument can justify. First, the labor has to be above and beyond what morality requires a person to do for others. And that can be a very large condition indeed under some circumstances. For morality not only requires the fulfillment of obligations, but the exemplification of at least some moral character traits and occasional concessions to the principle of maximizing goods. Morality encourages and permits much else, but it *requires* that much – at least in the sense that not to do it makes one liable for reprobation.[16] And though others may not 'deserve' the benefits morality requires one to confer on them, it is none the less wrong to withhold them. When excluding others from the fruits of one's labor amounts to withholding such benefits from others, then such withholding cannot be justified – at least not by the labor argument alone.

The supplemental value requirement. Second, the labor must produce something which would not have existed except for it. This restriction is simply designed to call attention to the difference between the land one labors on and what is produced. Under some circumstances (such as the draining of a swamp, the filling of an estuary, etc.), one may fairly claim that one's labor has produced usable land itself. But under most circumstances, it is not the land itself that labor produces, but something *from* the land. Similarly for the water in a well, stream, or lake. The entitlement to labor's products cannot extend (except by convention) to the means of production – at least to the extent that the means of production are not themselves the products of labor.

The no-loss requirement. Third, the property rights to which one acceeds by virtue of labor must not constitute a loss to others. Many disputes about the legitimacy of property rights can be understood as veiled disagreements about the interpretation of this requirement. If it is taken to mean that no one must be put at a relative disadvantage by another's accession to property rights, then it is doubtful whether one could legitimately claim ownership of any significant product of one's labors. Even a toothbrush, in so far as it is an advantage, puts its possessor in a position of relative superiority over those who do not possess one.

But surely this stretches the concept of a 'loss' too far. The point of this restriction is to exclude a laborer's taking away others' existing goods. Equality of bad teeth is not an existing good, except in competitive situations where good teeth are a competitive advantage. So I have not 'taken away' a good from others by my possession of a toothbrush. Land and the means of production, however, are a different matter. No doubt unused land represents a benefit to people only in so far as it is an opportunity of one sort or another. None the less, the elimination of those opportunities by the acquisition of land which does not leave 'enough and as good' for others *is* a loss to those others. The point of Locke's restriction, as applied to land and finite non-renewable resources generally, is clear on this issue. (Its application to cases, of course, will depend largely on the explication of what it means to leave 'enough' for others. And this will be a difficult problem indeed for any society which is [in any sense] overpopulated, or in which an equal sharing of some available resource would mean that the most industrious would get significantly less than they could use.)

There is still a large conflict, however, between the way various anti-property theorists might regard the notion of a 'loss' and the explication just given. In a competitive situation, it will be urged, to be put at a competitive disadvantage is a loss in precisely the way the inability to acquire land is a lost opportunity. And acquisition of property rights which puts others at a competitive disadvantage is therefore a 'taking away' of an existing good' — namely, competitive parity.

It seems to me that this is correct, and that it does not, like the concept of relative disadvantage, stretch the notion of a 'loss' beyond recognition. There may be nothing 'good' about having teeth as rotten as your neighbor's. Thus when he improves his relative to yours, the equality lost is not necessarily the loss of a good. But in a competitive situation the loss of competitive equality, or any deterioration of one's competitive position, *is* necessarily the loss of a good.

The extent to which the principle of entitlement to the fruits of one's labor can justify property rights is thus greatly limited in *competitive situations* — so much so, I suspect, as to defeat most of the point of Locke's arguments. In competitive situations, the restrictions on ownership must be extended to at least the major means of production. Locke's argument then becomes a foundation for socialism rather than 'possessive individualism.' Land, other natural resources, and the major means of production (sources of energy, transportation, communication, heavy industry, and important tools or knowledge too difficult for the individual to manufacture from available resources), cannot be privately owned. If they are acquired privately, they either deprive others of opportunity, or put them at a competitive disadvantage. In either case the requirement that no one suffer loss by the producer's acquisition of property is violated.

Entitlement reconsidered

It will surely be urged in reply, however, that there is something very wrong with this explication of the root idea of the labor theory. Proudhon's attack boils down to 'I didn't ask you to work, so I should not

have to pay you in the form of property rights for the work you did.'
Mill's reply is, 'As long as it is no loss to you − no "payment" − why
should you care?' All this is very well as rhetoric, it will be said, but
when the consequences of Mill's reply themselves undermine the
theory, something is wrong. For after all, why *shouldn't* the industrious
gain competitive advantages over the non-industrious? Locke himself
remarks that '[God] gave [the earth] to the use of the industrious and
rational. . .'[17] He clearly had it in mind that there could be no justice
in a system which did not distinguish, in the distribution of goods,
between the producers of those goods and the non-producers. But why
is this so? It cannot be for the reason that Mill gives (that the inequality
constitutes no loss to the unindustrious), for whenever they are thereby
put at a competitive disadvantage, they do suffer a loss. And to say that
the producers *deserve* the property because they earned it with their
labor is just to repeat, with emphasis, the original premise − the root
idea of the labor theory one is trying to explicate.

Further, when the reply here is taken out of the language of the
work ethic and one substitutes for 'industrious' the terms (equally
accurate as things actually happen) 'aggressive,' 'intelligent,' and
'strong,' and substitutes for 'unindustrious' the terms 'passive,' unintel-
ligent,' and 'weak,' the reply loses some appeal. Why should the aggressive inherit the earth, after all? They have, but has it been a good thing?
Why should the people with the natural advantage of intelligence
(whether acquired by inheritance or by environment) inherit the earth?
Have they *earned* the means which permit their acquisition? And so on.

(It should be noted that the social Darwinist rationale for the right
of the strong to the advantages conferred by property reduces to an
absurdity. As Rashdall points out, property rights − especially when
they protect possession and inheritance − quite clearly protect the
weak against the strong.[18])

The final blow to the argument is this: it may be that in some situations a laborer's accession to liberty rights is no loss to others, but the
accession to a *claim right,* or a power, or an immunity, is usually a
different matter. The creation of the corresponding duties, liabilities,
and disabilities in others usually constitutes a loss of *liberty* for them.
Rights justified by this argument cannot, then, include claim rights,
powers, or immunities *if and in so far as* the existence of those sorts of
rights actually constitutes a loss to others. And all of the varieties of
ownership distinguished at the outset involve not only liberties but
claim rights or powers or immunities as well.

Yet even when all this is said, it must be admitted that a person's
commitment to the root idea of the labor theory may not have been

disturbed very much by the argument so far. Head shaking, protestations that the analysis has 'gone too fast' or must have overlooked some alternatives, and general carping about the poverty of philosophy are more typical reactions. This is not an unusual result when an analysis has been unable to find rational support for a widely held moral conviction. But the persistence of the conviction after all this is enough to give one cause to consider another possibility: that the whole effort to find arguments to justify the labor theory may have been wrongheaded.

Laborer's entitlement as a fundamental principle. Suppose it is urged that one should not try to go behind the root idea of the labor theory at all — that this root idea is just a fundamental or primitive moral principle which neither needs nor is capable of justification. Once this suggestion is made, the argument shifts to the issue of what it means to say that a moral idea is primitive or fundamental, and the justification for thinking that the labor theory contains such an idea.

Now there are several senses in which an idea may be said to be so fundamental as to defy moral justification. First, an idea may so permeate the whole 'moral conceptualization' of the world that to discard it would be to discard altogether the enterprise of making moral judgments. The notion that agents are responsible for their acts has been thought to be this sort of fundamental idea, as has the generalizability of moral judgments. 'Going behind' either of these ideas to talk about their moral justifiability might thus be held to be circular; they are simply constitutive of the concept of morality *per se.*

Second, an idea may be necessary to the conceptualization of an important range of cases *within* moral life — necessary in the sense that without it one loses one's grip on the particular moral problem the cases present. The concept of desert might be thought fundamental in this way to the problem of penalties and punishment (as opposed to reformation or deterrence). Without it, one hardly knows how to proceed. Thus it might be urged that in a discussion of restorative or retributive justice the justifiability of the notion that people can deserve certain things is assumed. One treats that notion as fundamental and does not go behind it; it is just constitutive of the concept under discussion.

Third, an idea may be regarded as fundamental in the sense that it is the best choice of the alternatives available for a justificatory 'starting point.' Justifications cannot prove everything; they have to start somewhere — with something which is itself unproved. The best starting point, of course, is one which is indisputable. But for anything beyond purely formal systems, it is hard to find indisputable axioms. Instead, one must usually settle for something which is not actually *in* serious dispute and which can otherwise perform the role of an axiom (for example, axioms must be self-consistent, be stated clearly and unambiguously, and be suitably powerful or 'at the bottom' of many justificatory issues).

I think it is clear that the root idea of the labor theory cannot qualify as fundamental in either of the first two senses: there is no logical circularity involved in asking for a moral justification of it, and it is certainly not presupposed by the conceptualization of the problems raised by the justification of property rights (witness ancient discussions of property acquisition). So we are left with the possibility that it may be fundamental in the third sense — that is, that it is the best (or a member of the best set of) justificatory 'starting point(s).'

This contention has some initial plausibility. The general, unquestioning approval of the idea is a modern (Western?) phenomenon, but one which is very firmly established. So the condition that the starting point not actually be in dispute seems satisfied. Further, the idea that laborers are entitled to the products of their labor seems (initially) to satisfy some of the other requirements of an axiom: generality; self-consistency; the ability to generate determinate conclusions when applied to cases. But in each case this initial plausibility crumbles upon inspection.

For example, if there is general agreement that laborers should get property rights in the fruits of their labor, there is also general agreement that this should not be at the expense of others. Proudhon's challenge, 'I did not ask you to work so why should I have to pay you for what you did?' is as generally agreed to as the root idea of the labor theory. That is surely part of the reason Locke and Mill were so careful to include the 'no loss' requirement in their arguments. So any attempt to treat the root idea as a plausible first principle *on the basis of people's actual commitment to it* would, if it were to be consistent, have to include a qualification equivalent to the 'no loss' requirement. Thus nothing would have been gained by treating the root idea as a first principle (since with the no loss requirement, its justification goes through anyway).

Further, there is an insuperable problem with the generality of the idea. Laborers are supposed to be entitled to property in the *very things* they produce (and where these are inseparable from the raw materials worked on, property in the things worked on). But it has already been shown that this supposition must be revised in the case of the children parents produce. And it is equally clear that it will not do for the whole class of employees and the equally large class of people who perform services for others. It is perhaps true that most employees work on things already owned by others, and since labor is only claimed to be a mode of original acquisition, for that reason they cannot come to own the very things they produce or work on. But why is it not generally agreed that scholars have property rights in the ideas they produce (as opposed to the books the ideas are published in)? Surely it is not because the ideas are owned by someone else. Nor is it because scholars do not claim those ideas as 'their own,' for they do so claim them. Nor is it because scholars have all waived possible property rights prior to beginning to work (as might be the case for certain government or corporate employees engaged in research), for some of them have not done so. Why, in short, is it sometimes generally agreed that people should have property rights in their ideas (in the form of copyrights and patents), but not always? And why is it generally accepted that patents and copyrights lapse automatically after a period of time, while ownership of land acquired by labor would not be expected to?[19] *Once it is acknowledged that some labor is expected to yield property rights in the very things labored on, while other labor is not,* the root idea of the labor theory must be seen as a poor choice for a fundamental principle. In the form in which it can claim general acceptance, it simply does not 'cover' all the cases. The obvious covering principle is that laborers *deserve* something for their labor. Perhaps in some cases what they deserve is property in the thing labored on; in other cases property in some sort of fee for the labor; and in still other cases, not property at all but simply the recognition, admiration, or gratitude of other people. If the principle of desert can settle when people deserve property rights in the products of their labor, then we will have a plausible reformulation of the labor theory (see below, pp. 48ff). But we should be clear that it will be a reformulation, not the traditional version.

The upshot of this is, then, that the Locke—Mill labor theory cannot serve as a fundamental, unjustified moral principle. If any principle related to labor has that status it is the notion that labor should be rewarded. This principle may in some cases justify recognizing a property right in the thing labored on. In other cases, it may not. In any case, to repeat, it is not the root idea of the labor theory of property acquisition — at least as traditionally formulated — which is at the bottom of such justifications.

Fair taking: a final note. It is one thing to tell people they ought to give away things they have produced; it is quite another to tell them the things are not theirs to give. It is one thing to tell people that they ought not to take unfair advantage of others; it is another thing to tell them that they are not entitled to advantages taken fairly. And there is still something so far unsaid about the 'fair taking' idea.

Proudhon's objections, and Mill's reply, concern situations in which people go about producing things wholly on their own — without being asked, and without initial reference to the desires, needs, or abilities of others. *Then* it is asked: how does their labor justify rights to what they produce? The answer, naturally enough, is in terms of objections people might raise against the producers. 'You have destroyed *my* opportunities for acquisition.' Or, 'You have put me at a disadvantage.'

But suppose we imagine a situation in which there are enough resources (initially) for each person to make full use of his or her abilities, people are equal in ability, and aware of the consequences for their own eventual opportunities and competitive positions if they allow others to 'get ahead.' This, I think, is the sort of picture last-ditch defenders of the labor theory conjure up. What, they ask, is wrong with securing for the industrious the fruits of their labor in that sort of situation? It is true that they will soon have a competitive advantage over the idlers, but so what? Surely they deserve it. And if their initial acquisitions make it possible for them to use more of the land, minerals, and other resources than they could initially, and the non-producers see this, but still do not care to appropriate (by their labor) their original 'shares,' then what is unfair about letting the industrious take that too?

It must be granted that in the situation just described, the slothful do not deserve the produce of others. Nor do they deserve to be protected from the consequences of their own sloth (conditions justifying paternalism having been ruled out). And so it would not be wrong to give property rights — including claim rights — to the industrious. But this is hardly a comfort to the defenders of the labor theory. In the first place it is still too weak: at best, one can only derive a recipient right from it, and that is not a property right. Second, as described, the situation in which one can take advantage 'fairly' is so rare as to be of very little practical importance beyond certain special colonizing enterprises.[20] Third, the 'fairness' of the situation is wrecked with the arrival of the second generation. Even if inheritance is not permitted, the members of the first generation and those of the second who come to maturity first clearly leave the remainder, no matter how industrious, with reduced opportunities. So the 'industrious colonist' metaphor does not advance the range of allowable property rights very far.

Deserving to own: reformulating the labor theory
One is left, again, with little more than the persistence of the root idea — and the vehemence of its advocates. One explanation for this may be

found in a psychological fact: that labor is (in some circumstances) *psychological* appropriation – appropriation in the sense of a 'felt incorporation' of the thing labored on 'into' one's person. If it is true that I 'am' (psychologically) what I want to become as well as what I have become, then one can say with similar validity that I am what I have made. I am what I was, what I do, what I want to do, and what I produce. These are all greatly abbreviated locutions for complex facts about personality, but the ones which refer to the consequences of labor are no less sound than the others. The trouble is that while such facts may be able to support a claim for a recipient right, I see no way for them to go beyond that. It is not a happy situation.

I want, therefore, to explore one final possibility – the idea that there might be some principle of desert, related specifically to labor, which will satisfy the insistent demand that despite all the difficulties, something like the labor theory must be sound.[21] The idea is obviously very closely tied to Locke's notion of justice for those who 'take pains' or who add value to things by their own efforts, on their own initiative. But as far as I can tell, the argument to follow is not one that either Locke or Mill actually intended to make.

DESERT AS A FUNDAMENTAL PRINCIPLE

To begin, suppose we acknowledge that the notion of desert is a constituent of the notion of morality *per se*. This may not be immediately obvious, but consider: Morality is concerned with (among other things) questions of what people ought to do and be. And among the things which people ought to do and be it is certainly held that there are some moral requirements – that is, things for which sanctions of various sorts will be invoked if people fail to do what they ought, or fail to be what they ought. (There may be other things which are morally good or bad but which are not either required or forbidden.) Now it is understood that, by definition, moral sanctions – reprobation, blame, punishment, and their opposites – are not just instrumental acts, to be invoked whenever they will yield a desirable result. They are to be applied only to those who 'deserve' or are 'worthy' of the sanction. One must be morally blame*worthy,* or praise*worthy* for it to be appropriate for a moral sanction to be imposed. Thus just as surely as the notion of moral requirements and prohibitions (and the concomitant sanctions) necessarily involves the notion of agents who can be said to be responsible for their acts, so too it necessarily involves the notion of desert. To ask whether desert is an intelligible concept is to call into question the whole enterprise of passing moral judgment on people for their conduct. If agents can be morally responsible for their acts, they can by definition deserve reward or punishment for them. That is part of what it means to say someone is a responsible agent. And if they cannot deserve moral sanctions, they cannot be morally responsible for their conduct. The whole enterprise of making moral judgments is indefensible. Unless we are wholesale moral sceptics, then, we have to acknowledge the intelligibility — indeed the necessity — of the concept of moral desert.

But what does deserving something mean? That is, what 'principles of moral desert' can be articulated simply by analyzing the concept itself? Here Joel Feinberg's careful analysis is useful.[22] First, it is clear that claims that people deserve this or that must have a 'basis.' That is, '[i]f a person is deserving of some sort of treatment, he must, necessarily, be so *in virtue* of some possessed characteristic or prior activity . . . Of course, [one] may not know the basis of [another's] desert, but if [one] denies that there is any basis, then he has forfeited the right to use the terminology of desert.'[23]

The basis for a desert-claim, however, is to be distinguished from the basis for a claim that a person is eligible, or qualified, or entitled to something (where entitled means having a claim right to a thing).[24] And the basis for a desert-claim must, in general, be some fact about the person who is said to be deserving. One can imagine a case in which one *ought* (morally) to reward X simply because it would make X's parents very happy; but that is not a basis for saying that X *deserves* a reward.[25]

What is a basis for a desert-claim? Happily, we need not be able to give a comprehensive answer to that question to see that, by definition again, personal deeds and character *may* be bases. We sometimes give reasons for *not* using them. ('I suppose it was "good" of him to return the money, but after all he owed it to me. People don't deserve anything special for doing their duty.') But we do not normally give reasons *for* using personal deeds and character as desert bases because what else, after all, could be a basis for *personal* desert? So it must be the case that a person's 'adding value' to the world — in the sense of discovering, inventing, or improving something which helps others — *can* be a basis for a desert-claim. And once we add the stipulations that the deed be both morally permissible and beyond what is morally required of the person, I cannot imagine any objection to the assertion that such 'adding of value' *must* be a basis for a desert-claim. Then, finally, since the very notion of personal desert is that 'good things' (prizes, rewards, benefits) are what befit good deeds or good character (when they are desert bases), the following principle must be sound simply by definition:

A person who, in some morally permissble way, and without

being morally required to do so, 'adds value' to others' lives deserves some benefit for it.[26]

I have gone over these definitional matters with no doubt tedious care because philosophers have been justifiably leary of the notion of desert. I do not want to leave the impression that anything has been hidden. For I now want to claim to have shown that the desert principle just ennunciated meets the requirements for a fundamental principle of the first sort (above, p. 45). It certainly also meets the requirements for the other two sorts (pp. 45-6). It does this, in short, because the concept of desert is constitutive of the concept of morality *per se,* and because the principle of desert given above is entailed by that very concept of desert.

SOME FEATURES OF THIS PRINCIPLE OF DESERT

Once this much is granted, there are several things which can be said immediately about this principle of desert. In the first place, it must be a double-edged principle: if a benefit is due for adding value, presumably a penalty is due for subtracting value. Such symmetry is a conceptual requirement for *this* principle of desert (though not for all), because the context in which the concept of desert here operates calls for a 'polar' notion of desert.[27] 'Adding value' is taken to be a good deed; good deeds have their opposites. (Here that would mean 'subtracting value.') If benefits are what befit good deeds, penalties are what befit bad ones. The principle of desert stated here cannot consistently affirm the former without also affirming the latter. On the assumption that there are some morally permissible acts which both add and subtract values — by improving the lot of some at the expense of others — then it follows that sometimes both a benefit and a penalty are due. This results in an argument for a tax on entrepreneurs whose activities deplete the community's stock of unowned resources or limit the opportunity of others without their consent; and it results in an argument for compensation to any persons who suffer a demonstrable net personal loss. The size of such penalties may in effect cancel the benefit entirely, of course.

Second, we must hold the principle of desert to be totally inapplicable to cases in which gains are gotten by violating moral prohibitions — e.g. by unjustifiably overriding the rights of others. And this is so no matter how much more good than bad is eventually produced. It is, after all, a principle of personal desert being considered, and if the balance of good over bad does not justify overriding the right, then it is hardly consistent to think that the wrongdoer deserves a benefit for whatever good is done. Consider immoral medical experiments on unwilling human subjects. (The case is different for rights which are justifiably overridden. Compensation is still due, but the notion of desert is applicable.)

Third, the desert principle must include a proportionality requirement: Benefit or penalty to be proportional to the value added or subtracted by the labor. I say for the value produced rather than for the (value of the) labor expended, for conceptual reasons. By the terms of the desert principle as stated, value accrued or lost without labor does not count. Labor is a necessary condition for desert. But it is not sufficient. Labor alone — labor which neither adds to nor diminishes value — does not deserve anything. So the benefit must be proportional to the value produced by the labor (and if that is not separable from the total value of the product, then proportional to the total value of the product). Similarly, penalties are to be proportional to the loss produced by the labor.[28]

Fourth, and finally, the principle of desert must have a way of fitting the type of benefit to the type of labor or to the laborer. After all, a candy bar is not (usually) a fitting reward for someone who does not like sweets.

I suggest that each of these four elements must be regarded as a constitutive feature of the principle of desert under discussion. That is, the meaning of the principle of desert used here cannot be fully and self-consistently explicated without including them.

PROPERTY RIGHTS AS FITTING BENEFITS

It is the fourth element which raises the possibility for a new argument. Are there some types of labor for which property rights are the *only* fitting benefit? Or less strongly, are there some sorts of labor for which property rights are the *most* fitting benefits? (Care must be taken here not to let the standard for fittingness turn the argument into a version of the appeal to utility. For example, to argue that certain benefits are fitting because without them people would not do the things we want them to do is to give a utility argument, not a labor-desert argument. The standard of fittingness must come instead from the nature of the labor, the laborer, or the products of labor. And it is not immediately obvious how this will work.)

Suppose we begin by recalling once again that labor (as opposed to random expenditure of effort and play) is goal-directed activity. It is undertaken for some purpose — for the satisfaction of some desire. Now, it is clear that the satisfaction of some such desires might in principle require property rights, while the satisfaction of others does not. If the whole purpose (or an indispensable part of the purpose) of the laborer's efforts is to get and keep as property what the labor produces, then if the laborer deserves a benefit for his or her efforts, and if property rights in the thing produced do not exceed the proportionality requirement, then they are obviously the only (or part of the only) fitting benefit.

Note that this does not mean that people can come to deserve property rights by simply having them as part of their goals when they undertake to do something. What they do must deserve a benefit, and a benefit of a size comparable to the value of the property rights they want (whether full, liberal ownership or some more restricted variety). Once this is understood, the labor-desert argument looks quite sound. Further, the use of the goal of labor as the mark against which to measure the fittingness of benefits allows for an account of why and when money rewards can be susbstituted for rights to the very thing produced. For example, if my object in gardening is to have the satisfaction of eating things I have grown, then substitutes (like money to buy other produce) won't do. On the other hand, if all I want is vegetables of a certain quality, at certain times, at a certain convenience, then it may well be a matter of indifference whether my entitlement is to property in the very things I have produced or to money to buy equivalent products.

Similarly for the issue of when, and why, the recognition, admiration, and gratitude of one's peers are more fitting than either money or property in the thing produced. Some things, after all, are not done for fortune. They may be done for fame, for example. One may want to be admired — known for something. In that case, reward of money and anonymity is a poor substitute for what is sought. (Think of James Watson's desire to be the first to understand DNA.[29])

THE LABOR–DESERT ARGUMENT FOR PROPERTY

What does this mean for private property rights? Well, it means that when people deserve a benefit for their labor, and when (in terms of the purposes of their efforts) nothing but property in the things produced will do, and when the value of such rights meets the test of proportionality, then they deserve property in those things. When, on the other hand, substitutes will do every bit as well, they then deserve either the things produced or an equally satisfactory substitute. And finally, where property in the things produced is not what is sought at all, and cannot be an adequate substitute for what is sought, the laborers deserve something else (perhaps recognition, gratitude).

Put more formally, this version of the labor argument is as follows:

(1) When it is beyond what morality requires them to do for others, people deserve some benefit for the value their (morally permissible)

53

labor produces, and conversely, they deserve some penalty for the dis-value their labor produces.

(2) The benefits and penalties deserved are those proportional to the values and disvalues produced, and those fitting for the type of labor done.

(3) When, in terms of the purposes of the labor, nothing but property rights in the things produced can be considered a fitting benefit for the labor, and when the benefit provided by such rights is proportional to the value produced by the labor, the property rights are deserved;

when, in terms of the purposes of the labor, either property rights in the things produced or something else can be considered a fitting and proportional benefit, then either the property rights or one of the acceptable alternatives is deserved;

when, in terms of the purposes of the labor, property rights in the things produced cannot be considered a fitting reward, or when the benefits of such rights is in excess of the values produced by the labor, the rights are not deserved.

(4) Any diminution of value produced by labor must be assessed against the laborer as a penalty deserved for the loss thus produced. (Penalties must, of course, be proportional to the loss produced, and a fitting remedy for that loss — fitting not in terms of the purposes of the labor which produced it, but in terms of the purposes with regard to which it can be considered a loss.)

It should be noted that (1) meets the standards for a fundamental principle of the sorts explicated above (pp. 45ff), and the remaining steps are deduced from the concepts of desert, fittingness, benefit, and loss. I think this line of argument is sound, and is in fact what the labor theory reduces to. I think, further, that it satisfies the stubborn desire we have to make the labor theory work. But several things should be noted about what it does and does not prove.

In the first place, this labor argument — by itself — gives no unequivocal grounds for the private ownership of the things produced unless there is no substitute for it acceptable in terms of the goals of the labor. This means that where the production of things is a means to an end — security, power, status, the ability to guarantee the same for one's children, etc. — and where the state can provide those things *as laborers' deserts* without granting ownership rights over the very things produced, this version of the labor theory does not provide a justification for private ownership of the things produced. It is thus in principle compatible with socialist economic arrangements.

Second, the no-loss requirement — here understood as the double-edged aspect of the desert principle — places a heavy tax and/or compensation requirement on entrepreneurs whose activities reduce total welfare, or opportunities, or which otherwise disadvantage their fellows. But here it can be seen that the type of thing produced has a great deal to do with such restrictions. For one thing, the problems with 'intellectual property' become clearer. In the case of technological problems for which there is a unique solution (or a very small, well-defined class of solutions), an invention by one person — if it is then fully owned by that person — significantly diminishes the opportunities of others. We therefore have grounds for sharply limiting or taxing patent and copyright arrangements, just as we have grounds for limiting or taxing the acquisition of land and exhaustible natural resources generally. On the other hand, we have no grounds for penalizing someone *just because* he or she has invented or created something unique. Inventions *per se* do not diminish the net number of opportunities to invent *other* things, any more than the writing of *Moby Dick* diminished the opportunities of subsequent novelists. The classes of possibilities are not finite. And in the case of art, each work, by its very existence, creates new possibilities — for further work which 'refers to' or 'uses' it, for example.

Third, it should be noticed that the labor—desert argument does nothing to establish entitlement in cases where the laborer's efforts have not benefitted anyone else. Deserving a benefit for producing something which only you profit from is a strange notion. So the applicability of the argument is confined to cases in which the product of one's labor itself (independently of whether one owns it) adds value to others' lives. Cases in which others are neither benefitted nor harmed by the labor (e.g. by one's use of some nonscarce sand to make an hourglass purely for personal amusement) must be dealt with in terms of the Locke-Mill version of the labor theory. See above, pp. 41ff.

Fourth, and finally, there is a strange result of this line of argument which demands notice. If the fittingness of a reward is tied only to the satisfaction of the laborer's purposes, then what is to be done by way of rewarding people whose purpose is *just* to work, *just* to produce useful or beautiful things, or to discover the truth about things? Whether or not anyone ever works solely for such motives, surely many people often work partly for them. Is such labor to be its own reward entirely, just because the laborers do not happen to want more? Or is there some additional way of justifying the fittingness of (an additional) reward?

It is here, of course, that honors, recognition, gratitude, and status rewards are often used. And the fittingness of these rewards (as well as other benefits) is no more difficult to understand than the appropriateness of returning love with love and kindness with kindness. Other responses are simply not compatible with our ideals of moral character.

However one argues for the justifiability of an ideal (whether solely on utilitarian grounds or not), it would not be easy, I think, to defend a notion of the good person which entailed a disposition to treat hatred or indifference as an appropriate response to another's love, or vindictiveness, disgust or apathy as an appropriate response to another's kindness.[30] In short, we need not fear that this principle of desert — this version of the labor theory — will shortchange the selfless.

To summarize, then, this tortuous analysis of the labor theory: the version proposed by Mill — with the no-loss requirement as explicated here — is sound, but of very limited applicability in its traditional form. It works most satisfactorily in the case of the sorts of personal possessions (e.g. a small rock collection) whose ownership harms no one. When reformulated with the desert principle, however, the labor theory possesses most of the power of the original intuition. This does not mean that the no-loss requirement has been relaxed. Indeed, the penalty clause of the desert principle provides a strong ground for tax and compensation requirements on entrepreneurs. But the re-interpretation provided by the desert principle at last allows a clear account of why and when laborers — solely by virtue of their labor, and not just because there are no objections to it — deserve to own what they produce.

5 Arguments from Utility

There are two major variants of utility arguments for property rights. Both assert that property rights are necessary as a means to an end — the end being human happiness. But in one variant — what I shall call *traditional* utility arguments — happiness is defined very broadly, so as to include the whole range of human satisfactions. The other variant — what I shall call *economic* utility arguments — defines happiness more narrowly; it concerns only those satisfactions which can be sought by economic transactions and measured by 'dollar votes.' The two variants are fully compatible; in fact, the economic arguments are special cases of traditional appeals to utility. I shall give the two variants separate exposition here, however, because there has been a tendency in legal and economic writing to overlook or dismiss traditional arguments, and to give economic arguments a logical primacy they do not deserve.

The traditional arguments

(1a) Human beings need some rule-governed social institutions in order to achieve (the means to) a reasonable degree of happiness.

(1b) Some specific institutions are necessary for the achievement of happiness; others are merely useful, or not useful; still others inhibit or prevent the achievement of happiness.

(1c) Which institutions are necessary is to be determined by an examination of the social conditions which are required for happiness but which cannot exist without rule-governed institutions. (Similarly, *mutatis mutandis,* for institutions which are useful, useless, or detrimental for achieving happiness.)

(1d) How those necessary institutions are to be defined is to be determined by how well the rules (and principles, policies, and practices) constitutive of their various possible definitions, when applied to cases,

57

meet the needs which make the institution necessary. (Similarly, *mutatis mutandis,* for the definition of useful, useless, and detrimental institutions.)

(1e) People need individually to acquire, possess, use, and consume some things in order to achieve (the means to) a reasonable degree of happiness.

(1f) Security in possession and use is impossible (given human society as we know it) unless enforced and unless modes of acquisition are controlled. Such control and enforcement amounts to the administration of a system of property rights.

(1g) Insecurity in possession and use, and uncontrolled acquisition, of the goods people need and want makes an individual's achievement of (the means to) a reasonable degree of happiness impossible (or very unlikely).

(1h) Therefore, a system of property rights is necessary (or very nearly so) if individuals are to achieve (the means to) even a reasonable degree of happiness.

That, in outline, is the general justification for property rights from 'utility.' There are also utility arguments at the levels of specific and particular justification. The specific form is this: Assuming the general form of the argument, one takes premises (a) through (d) and adds:

(2e) Concerning the needed system of property rights, people need, or persistently want, the following sorts of property rights. . . .

(2f) Denying people what they need or what they persistently want, without a showing that the denial is necessary for some countervailing good, is unjustifiable (and usually productive of social disorder and further governmental repression as well).

(2g) Therefore, when there is no countervailing good to consider, people should be permitted the sorts of property rights they need and persistently want.

The particular form is more direct. It simply asserts that:

(3a) It would be best on balance for society as a whole, if X had property right of sort A in thing T.

(3b) If there are no countervailing reasons to the contrary, one should do what is best, on balance, for society as a whole.

(3c) Therefore, if there are no countervailing reasons to the contrary, X should have a property right of sort A in thing T.

These arguments from utility are among the oldest, and certainly most frequently given, justifications of private ownership. They have the advantages of directness and (apparent) simplicity: in schematic form, they are deductively valid; and they seem more 'realistic' than talk about natural acquisition in some fictional state of nature.

Yet most of their proponents agree that such utility arguments no more reflect the actual origins of property than do theories of first occupancy and labor;[1] explications of the arguments are usually themselves embedded in state-of-nature theory; and when one begins to examine their premises in detail, their apparent simplicity largely disappears.

Still, these arguments from utility are central to the justification of property rights. If this general form of the argument cannot provide at least a partial rationale for the institution, it is doubtful if anything can. It is not that there are no other lines of argument; there are. But a negative result here would conflict with the attempt to justify property on other grounds — and might overwhelm those other grounds. A careful analysis of the arguments is thus required.

Analysis of the traditional arguments

It is useful to begin by noting that these three utility arguments are not designed to justify the mere protection of possession, use, management, and so forth, but the corresponding *rights*. That is, taken together, the arguments are addressed to the justification of a set of rules, policies, principles, and practices constitutive of a social institution which defines rights of ownership, as well as specifies the conditions under which one may obtain those rights, and the things which may be owned. They are thus a schema for a comprehensive account, not only of the fundamentals of the institution of property, but of its details as well.

THE NEED FOR INSTITUTIONS

The first three premises of the general argument address, respectively, the need for institutions, the necessity of some, and the method of determining which are necessary. They are not always sharply separated in presentations of the argument, but they present importantly distinct issues.

The first premise presupposes agreement that the achievement, by humans, of a reasonable degree of happiness is a fundamental good — fundamental enough so that if anything is necessary to its achievement, a very powerful counterargument would be needed to prove that that thing ought not to be permitted. (Obviously, utilitarians typically make much stronger claims for human happiness as a good, but this is all the current argument requires. And since to use a stronger claim would involve needless controversy, the weakest version possible will be used.) I shall assume that this weak presupposition about the good of human happiness needs no defense — short of an answer to thoroughgoing moral scepticism.[2]

The first premise, then, asserts that we need some rule-governed social institutions to achieve a reasonable degree of happiness — or at least to achieve the means to such happiness. There are various arguments used to establish such a need. Hume remarks that humans, among all animals, seem to be singularly unfortunate, due to the 'numberless wants and necessities' they have and the 'slender means' nature provides to relieve them. Only by forming societies are we able to supply our needs at all adequately.

> Society provides a remedy for these *three* inconveniences. By
> the conjunction of forces, our power is augmented: By the
> partition of employments, our ability increases. And by
> mutual succour we are less expos'd to fortune and accidents.
> 'Tis by this additional *force, ability,* and *security,* that society
> becomes advantageous.[3]

It is clear that the only effective way of organizing aggregates of people into societies capable of 'conjunction of forces,' 'partition of employments,' and 'mutual succour' is to enlist them in ongoing social institutions. The need to control violence, to predict others' conduct enough so that one can plan and carry out purposes which involve their cooperation, and the need to transmit knowledge all provide bases for the assertion of a need for social institutions.

THE NECESSITY FOR SOME INSTITUTIONS

Beyond the fact that some institutions are merely convenient or particularly efficient ways of meeting the needs noted above, the general argument from utility must establish that some institutions are *necessary* for the achievement of even a reasonable degree of happiness. The arguments for this premise are as familiar and uncontroversial as those for the first.

Hume puts matters most succinctly. He begins by listing three species of goods: 'the internal satisfaction of our minds, the external advantages of our body, and the enjoyment of such possessions as we have acquir'd by our industry and good fortune.'[4] All are necessary components in or means to happiness, and '[a]s the improvement, therefore, of these goods is the chief advantage of society, so the *instability* of their possession, along with their *scarcity,* is the chief impediment.'[5] This 'impediment' comes partly from some factors in our 'natural temper' (namely, selfishness, and limited generosity), and partly from some in our 'outward circumstances' (namely the 'easy change' and scarcity of external goods).

A long line of political and psychological theorists have presented a much bleaker picture of human nature, and have found the need for some social institutions — notably those directed toward the control of violence — even more compelling than Hume did. This line of theorists would have to include (though it surely did not begin with) Augustine, and go through many Christian theologians, as well as Machiavelli, Hobbes, and most modern psychologists and sociologists. Even those who believe that perfection in society means the absence of social institutions as defined here (e.g. perhaps Marx, probably classical anarchists) do not claim that such an arrangement is possible *given conditions as they have ever actually been.* This is enough to make the point needed for the argument from utility. Given the nature of human interactions as they actually occur, some social institutions are necessary for the achievement of a reasonable degree of happiness.

THE IDENTIFICATION OF THE NECESSARY INSTITUTIONS

Here the general argument from utility does not assert a premise which needs defense, but merely draws the only possible inference on the topic from the preceding two premises: that the necessary institutions are to be identified by examining the social conditions which are required for human happiness but which cannot exist without social institutions.

THE DEFINITION OF THE NECESSARY INSTITUTIONS

Similarly, the fourth step in the argument is merely a principle derived from the preceding three: that the particular character of a necessary institution must itself be submitted to the test of utility. If marriage is a necessary institution, then it has to be decided whether it is best defined to include polygamy or not. If property is found to be necessary, then questions will arise not only about the various ways of defining and limiting the scope of the incidents of 'full or liberal ownership,' but about including each of the incidents at all.

THE NEED TO ACQUIRE, POSSESS, USE, AND CONSUME

The fifth step in the general argument is the first to address any of the elements of property rights specifically. And there are several levels on which argument for this premise can proceed. First, there is the obvious fact, made a good deal of by Locke, for example,[6] that 'unappropriated' food does no one any good. Indeed, *unconsumable* food is of no use. Similarly for the other rudiments of bare existence. If they cannot be 'consumed,' then life itself, let alone happiness, is forfeited. To the extent that use and possession are necessary for consumption, they are as necessary to life and happiness as consumption.

People will readily agree, however, that something beyond these rudiments is required for human happiness — at least for the happiness of any human who has leisure and energy to spare from the work of survival. But what more? Specifically, what more in the way of acquisition, possession, use, and consumption of things? Here there are at least three lines of argument.

The first is simply that the application of minimal intelligence to the task of carrying out one's purposes shows the importance of the possession and use of things. Most purposeful activities require the use of tools and raw materials. And purposes which are at all long range require the continued availability of the necessary tools and materials. Possession of the means to carry out one's purposes allows one to predict with greater certainty the success of one's efforts. The absence of the necessary tools and materials, or their unavailability at crucial points in one's activities, frustrates the carrying out of one's purposes. To the extent that such frustration interferes with happiness, and to the extent that the acquisition, possession, use, and consumption of things reduces or eliminates such frustration, people need to acquire, possess, use, and consume. This is, I think, straightforward enough not to need further development here, and uncontroversial enough not to require further defense.

A second line of argument for the need to acquire, possess, and use assumes the need for an harmonious and stimulating social environment and argues that possession of things by individuals is superior to individual use of common possessions. Aristotle remarks that individual ownership creates a more thorough and stable community of interests, and better promotes efficient, economical, and careful use of things than does common ownership.[7] What is everyone's is felt to be no one's, and is so treated (i.e. with indifference).

In so far as this is simply a less rigorous version of an economic argument (to be presented below), it is food for thought. But while that economic argument is specifically limited to resource allocation, and does not even pretend to have provided a ground for full, liberal ownership, there may be a tendency to treat Aristotle's remarks as a sketch of a much more sweeping theory — one which justifies not only what might be called *laissez faire* private ownership, and not only ownership of productive resources, but ownership of (all or most) goods produced. Such an extension of the modern economist's argument about allocative transactions is unsound. It tends to confuse the absence of individual ownership rights with the absence of individual duties of care, for one thing. As long as the latter exist and are enforced, common property is well cared for. (The public libraries in most

Western democracies show this.) As for the community of interest issue, it is notorious that the 'community of interests' that property-holders develop is very often not in the interest of the community. So this can hardly be used to support a utilitarian argument. Finally, the economic disutilities which can result from untrammelled rights to transfer and to bequeath are notorious. A free market system is theoretically efficient only when competition is perfect (i.e. when it is without monopolistic or oligopolistic distortions of pricing mechanisms) and when transaction costs are zero (i.e. when it costs nothing to get the parties to a transaction to do what will actually maximize their welfare). There is general agreement among professional economists that one cannot expect to approximate efficiency in *every* area of the real market without *any* significant governmental intervention. Some such interventions, because they are designed to prevent market distortions caused by monopolies or oligopolies, will limit the rights to transfer and transmit. A sweeping justification for *laissez faire* private ownership from this line of argument is therefore not possible. As noted above, the argument does have force to the extent that private ownership is necessary or even merely beneficial to the general welfare. But I see no way of substantiating a claim for its universal necessity — or its unexcelled contribution to the general welfare in all cases.

The third and final line of argument for the need to acquire, possess, and use is more slippery. It centers on the claim that the acquisition, possession, and use of things is a necessary expression of human personality. Hegel made some remarks to this effect,[8] and it was a common theme among nineteenth-century idealists who addressed themselves to the topic.[9] There are two problems with this line: one is to get a clear, testable statement of its central assertion; the other is to test the truth of that assertion.

Suppose the central idea is put this way: Humans just are, necessarily, *makers*. For as far back as we have reasonably full records, it is clear that the normal course of maturation for a human individual in society has prominently involved the making or use of artifacts, and the transformation of things found (e.g. milk into cheese, wool into cloth). Such activities may or may not be biologically or psychologically necessary — that is, species characteristics — in the sense the sexual drive is. But they are certainly necessary in the sense that, for any normally formed human who comes to maturity in a human society of any kind which exists, is known to have existed, or could exist (given human potential as we know it) such activities necessarily play a dominant role in (a) the development of personality, self esteem, and valued abilities and (b) the subsequent expression of personality, the confirmation of self-esteem, and the use of valued abilities. These things are necessary to the achievement of (the means to) even a reasonable degree of happiness; the activities necessary to produce them are things necessary for happiness; and the acquisition, possession, and use of things is necessary to the activities which produce them. Thus humans need to acquire, possess, use, and consume (some) things.

I think this is a sound line of argument, but unfortunately it does little toward specifying the sorts of things people need to acquire, possess, and use. I shall return to this issue later.

SECURITY IN POSSESSION AND USE IS IMPOSSIBLE UNLESS ENFORCED AND UNLESS MODES OF ACQUISITION ARE CONTROLLED

On this premise there is sharp dissent from those who do not believe that coercive social institutions are necessary to all realizable social orders. Specifically, utopian Marxism proposes the 'withering away' of such institutions in a truly classless society. And various small-scale communal experiments (though by no means all) have tried to eliminate coercive institutions.

It is probably impossible, at present, to get more than a speculative argument on the issue. But some speculative arguments are reliable, and the following considerations seem to me decisive in favor of this premise in the argument from utility.

Where people have a genuine community of interests which at the same time is compatible with the interests of the community, where the habits of rational discussion and action on the basis of consensus are deeply ingrained in everyone, and where the community is small enough (or simple enough?) to permit life on such bases, the elimination of coercive institutions is no doubt possible. But where there is even one significantly deviant individual, or where individual conflicts of interest are not rationally resolvable by the parties concerned, or where the community is too large to submit all its major decisions to communal discussion, then it is difficult to see how coercive institutions could be eliminated altogether. And of course the notion of a modern industrial state, as we know it, without some such institutions, is preposterous.

Yet the question remains as to whether a coercive institution with respect to acquisition, possession, use, and consumption of things is necessary. Proponents of the utility argument say — as Hume does in the quotation which prefaces this book — that there is hardly any coercive institution which is more necessary in society. And certainly, given reasonable judgments about the selfishness of human beings, their limited generosity, and the relative scarcity of desirable goods available for acquisition, the utilitarians are correct. Whether in some imaginary utopia things might be different seems an academic question.

INSECURITY IN POSSESSION OR USE, AND UNCONTROLLED ACQUISITION, MAKE HAPPINESS IMPOSSIBLE

To the extent that a stable situation with regard to acquisition, possession, and use is required for the carrying out of purposes necessary to happiness, it follows that such a stable situation is itself necessary for happiness. If security of possession or use, and control of acquisition requires a system of property rights (as contended above) then property rights are needed which guarantee stability for as long as one's (necessary) purposes require. Security in possession required by long-term purposes will have to be long-term security, and so forth. Further, the sort of security required for the purposes will vary the property rights justified. The security required for the cultivation of land does not include the need to exclude people from walking across a fallow field. (Recall Grotius' discussion of 'innocent use.'[10]) But it is clear that some security, for some purposes, is necessary, given the soundness of the previous steps of the argument.

And there is an additional reason for requiring security of possession and control of acquisition. This is the fact, noted in the discussion of the labor theory, that people who work to acquire things, or who labor to make them more useful or pleasing, come to feel they have 'made them their own' in the psychological sense — that is, of having 'incorporated' or 'appropriated' them into themselves. The mark of this fact is the resentment felt and the responses made to the 'trespasses' of others. These reponses are virtually the same in kind, if not in intensity, as those people make to unwelcome 'touchings' of their bodies. This creates a need for stability in the possession of the products of one's labor above and beyond that required for the carrying out of one's (necessary for happiness) purposes. For the extent that freedom from the sense of resentment due to the 'violation' of one's person is necessary for happiness, then security in the possession and use of things one has 'appropriated' is a necessity.

THEREFORE, A SYSTEM OF PROPERTY RIGHTS IS NECESSARY

Given the soundness of the previous steps, the conclusion of the general form of the (traditional) argument from utility is deductively valid and itself sound.

As a general justification, however, the argument only produces the conclusion that some property rights in some things are necessary. What sorts of rights, over what sorts of things, has yet to be decided, and that requires the filling in of the specific form of the argument.

THE SPECIFIC FORM OF THE ARGUMENT

There are at least three important tasks involved in showing, by appeal to the traditional concept of utility, what sorts of property rights people should have.

First, one has to determine what sorts of things people need to acquire, possess, use, and consume in order to achieve (the means to) a reasonable degree of happiness. The list here will have to include the necessities for physical survival, personality development, and (certain) products of one's labor. But that is still not very specific, and how much beyond items in that list one can go is not clear.

Second, one needs to determine what sort of property rights are necessary (and best suited) to meet human needs. Must they always be the rights of 'full, liberal ownership'? Or will some subset of those rights do? And how must the various rights be defined to minimize conflicts and maximize security?

These two tasks constitute the filling in of premise (2e) of the specific argument. The third task is assuring the soundness of (2f). It asserts that denying people what they need or persistently want, in the absence of a showing that the denial is necessary for some countervailing good, is unjustifiable. This premise may seem stronger than it is. Actually, it presupposes only that giving people what they need or want is a good — in the sense that the satisfaction of any human need or want is a good. Once that is accepted, then it is tautological that *unless* there is some countervailing reason for denying people this good, its denial must be unjustifiable. The question which remains is whether giving people what they need (in this case) is a good. Their *having* it is by definition a good but that by itself does not entail that 'giving' it to them — in the form of creating social institutions which provide it — is a good. Here the general form of the argument enters: if such institutions are necessary for the satisfaction of the needs, then barring a countervailing concern (say, against the bad consequences of paternalism), the creation of the institution is justifiable.

THE PARTICULAR FORM OF THE ARGUMENT

As noted above, the soundness of the particular form of the traditional appeal to utility is somewhat independent of the soundness of the general and specific forms. A negative answer to the question of whether there should ever be any property rights at all is, of course, decisive with regard to particular justifications. If utility can *never* justify property rights, then attempts at particular justification are pointless.

But beyond that, particular justifications can cut through general and specific ones when it can be shown that, even though people generally ought not to have a certain sort of right, in a given case, people would be better off (or no worse off) if a particular person had such a right. Conversely, it can in principle happen that even though people in general *ought* to have a certain sort of right, in a given case people would be better off (worse off) if a particular person did not (did) have such a right.

Here the familiar problems of the relation of utility to justice arise. And they cannot be resolved by the (formal) device of smuggling the exceptions for particular cases into the general or specific principles. That move merely forces a restatement of the question: granted that these exceptions have utility, is it justifiable, all things considered, to make them? If, for example, making an exception improves the total (or the average) human welfare at the expense of enslaving a few, can one recommend such a course, all things considered? Are there not arguments for equal liberty which conflict with such a recommendation? If so, how is the conflict to be resolved?

The temptation to reach for the tools of welfare economics is strong here, but as I shall argue below, those tools are of less use than might have been hoped. The simplest — and I think best — *start* toward a solution is this: when faced with conflicting arguments, treat each as if it were of equal weight *unless there is good reason to do otherwise*. Then total the arguments. Two arguments (of equal weight) for human liberty outweigh one argument against it — and vice versa. Where there is a deadlock it means that none of the options is rationally preferred.

Two serious problems confront the use of this justificatory scheme: one is the question of assessing the reasons for weighting one argument more heavily than another (and of deciding how much heavier it is); the other is the question of the individuation of arguments (what counts as one argument?). I have addressed such questions elsewhere.[11]

The economic arguments
Dissatisfaction with traditional utility arguments — particularly with respect to the difficulty of measuring human happiness and the difficulty of interpersonal comparisons (what one person's happiness is worth compared to another's) — has led to attempts to make utility arguments more rigorous. Economists in particular have tried to do this, and have offered utility arguments for property rights at all three levels of justification.

The concept of value adopted by economists is simply the truism that whatever other values may be said to exist, a thing has value (utility) for a person when that person values it. (Whether things have 'intrinsic' worth, and whether some 'valuings' are better than others are questions which are left unaddressed.) *How much* value a thing has for a given person is said to be 'measured' by the maximum that person would be willing to pay to get it (in terms of some standard medium of exchange like dollars), or alternatively, the minimum the person would be willing to take to give it up.[12] Though this limits the range of values (utilities, satisfactions) considered to those which can in principle be exchanged and have a price, the assumption is that this will not be a serious difficulty for a discussion of property rights.

GENERAL JUSTIFICATION

Given this concept of value or utility, economists then offer two straightforward arguments for the general justifiability of a system of property rights. The first begins by noting the wide variety of costs or disutilities (in time, frustration of purpose, lost opportunities, etc.) which can befall one who depends on non-ownership use or enjoyment of a scarce good. Others can preempt one's uses, interfere with one's enjoyment, cause one to over-accumulate to offset anticipated losses, and so on. When the total cost of these 'external disutilities' – that is, the sum of the costs of the disutilities created for each by the actions of others – becomes greater than the costs involved in creating and maintaining a system of ownership rights which minimizes such externalities, then that system of property rights is justified by considerations of (economic) utility.[13] This argument is clearly sound, so long as the dominant guiding principle is one of minimizing costs.

The second general argument concerns allocative transactions – that is, the ways in which people deal with the resources used for the production of goods. Clearly, in a situation without enforced ownership rights, one would expect such transactions to be an uneasy amalgam of conduct in accordance with custom and social pressure, liberally laced with deceit, threats, and open force or violence. There is certainly no reason to believe that such transactions would maximize the total of individual satisfactions – either with respect to allocations or with respect to the eventual distribution of goods produced. And so, given the assumption that it is justifiable to maximize the total of satisfactions by tinkering with allocations, one step in that direction will be to stabilize allocative transactions with ownership rights. Richard Posner is thus able to argue briefly and persuasively for a system of property rights for all significantly scarce productive resources – a system which at least gives owners the right to exclude others as well as to transfer their rights.[14]

These arguments rest on some assumptions, to be sure — the principle of minimizing disvalues, and the justifiability of increasing benefits by stabilizing allocative transactions, respectively. But these assumptions are innocuous, since they do not claim to be the only relevant action-guiding principles but only ones which should be included in rational assessments of what to do. It is hard to see how they could be denied short of wholesale moral scepticism. So these two economic arguments buttress the general justification of property rights.

But in addition to these rather cautious arguments, a few economists have made a more sweeping claim: that private ownership and free markets are necessary for rational economic organization *per se* — whether that is understood simply in terms of maximizing the total of goods produced and consumed, or more complexly in terms of the maximization of what might be called Net Economic Welfare.[15] Members of the so-called Austrian School (Ludwig von Mises and F. A. Hayek, for example) have pressed such arguments. But socialists have plausible models too,[16] and I think it is fair to say that *at the level of general justification,* the debate is inconclusive. That is, I do not think that the Austrians can show, purely in terms of testable economic theory, that the socialization of a significant sector of the economy is, in every possible social order, impossible to justify; and likewise I do not think socialists can show that a sweeping system of private property is never justifiable. I take the fact that the overwhelming majority of modern economists argue for a mixed economy as evidence of this inconclusiveness. This is not to say that one or the other of these extreme positions cannot be made conclusive by the addition of further arguments — about what it is plausible to believe about human motivation, incentive, and competitiveness, for example, or about the amount of individual liberty or equality required by morality. But these matters take the arguments away from economic theory as such and into psychology, and normative moral and political philosophy. The sound *economic* utility arguments for the general justification of property rights remain the two rather cautious ones outlined above.

SPECIFIC JUSTIFICATION

Economic arguments for property rights take a somewhat different tack at the levels of specific and particular justification. Here they turn on technical concepts of efficiency, optimality, superiority, allocation, and distribution.

Economists distinguish the *allocation* of resources used for the production of goods (land, labor, etc.) from the *distribution* of goods produced. This distinction relates as much to a difference in human purposes as to a difference in the goods themselves, for the same things can often be used either as productive resources or 'consumables.' A good allocation is typically called *efficient;* a good distribution is typically called *just* or *fair.*

Efficient allocations and just distributions are defined by reference to special concepts of optimality and superiority — called Pareto-optimality and Pareto-superiority after the nineteenth-century Italian-born economist Vilfredo Pareto. A situation is said to be Pareto-optimal if and only if it is impossible to change it (in allocation or distribution) without making at least one person believe he is worse off than before the change. Derivatively, a change may be judged Pareto-superior to another when at least one person believes he is better off by it while *no one* believes that he is worse off. Note that the definitions of optimality and superiority do not depend on objective assessments of good, but only on subjective ones. This is an application of the economist's concept of value described earlier.

Whether people believe that they will be better off, worse off, or the same under any proposed change (and how much better or worse off they think they will be) is measured by their willingness to pay for the change (and how much), or to agree to it only if they are paid for it (and how much). One thus gets definitions of efficiency in resource allocation, for example, which go like this: a reallocation is efficient if, 'after negotiated compensations have been promised by those who stand to gain from the proposal to those who stand to lose by it, the proposal can win unanimous approval.'[17] A reallocation is also efficient, of course, if no one is either willing to pay for it or demands payment for it. Conversely, reallocations are inefficient to the extent that gainers from the change believe that they have to pay more than the gain is worth to them, or to the extent that losers believe that they cannot get adequate compensation for their loss. Justice or fairness in the redistribution of goods may be similarly defined: a redistribution is just when the price gainers are willing to pay equals the price losers are willing to accept (and the losers are paid that price).

Several things need to be said about the use of these definitions. In the first place they are embedded in an 'ideal market model' of economic transactions in which all participants are rational maximizers of their own values (utility, good, satisfactions), all participants are 'perfect competitors' (that is, none is able, by unilateral action, or by intentional multi-lateral action, to influence the price of goods), and in which transaction costs are zero (that is, in which it costs nothing to persuade others to behave rationally and come to know and act upon their own rational self-interests).

Second, when these materials have been used at the level of specific justification, they have been applied to a wide range of problems raised by property rights: liability rules governing the use of property,[18] zoning regulations,[19] and the issue of just compensation[20] are examples. As even a casual look at some of the legal materials will show,[21] there can be no hope here of dealing with these matters in adequate detail. But the fact that the same *patterns* of analysis are used in all these cases makes it possible to make some useful general observations about economic arguments for specific justification.

And third, for all their hard-headed appearance, it can easily be shown that when these materials are used to construct social policies with regard to property rights, most of the justificatory weight must be borne by non-economic or 'meta'-economic principles of a frankly normative sort – principles of justice, for example. This is not to denigrate the importance of economic analysis of these questions; it is merely to say that its results alone cannot settle the questions of specific justification.

To see this, consider what the fundamental form would be of an argument constructed from these economic materials alone:

(1) Property rights should be defined so as best to approximate, in operation, the idealized free market model of efficiency in allocation and justice in distribution.

(2) A perfectly free *real* market – i.e. one in which government only enforces whatever voluntary agreements people make – would clearly not have the character of the *ideal* free market. (Participants are not always perfect competitors and rational self-maximizers, and there are often significant transaction costs.)

(3) But it is an empirical question, in each case of a proposed intervention in the (real) free market, whether or not that intervention will move things closer to economic efficiency or justice as defined in the ideal free market model.

(4) So each proposal to limit property rights with liability rules, restrictions on use, transferability, transmissibility, possession, income or the rest of the elements of full ownership must be evaluated for its ability to move things toward efficient allocation and just distribution.

(5) When a proposed limitation of property rights would be no improvement on the real market (in terms of approximating the results of the ideal market), it cannot be justified; when a proposed change would be worse than the real market (in terms of approximating the results of the ideal market) it is 'wrong' – i.e. disjustified.

(6) Property rights of sort X best approximate the efficiency and justice of the ideal market in the real world and are therefore justified.

It is clear where problems with this form of argument arise. For one thing, efficiency and justice as here defined — while interesting and seemingly operationalizable concepts — are certainly contestable when put forward as social goals. However odd this may seem to some (what can be wrong with a situation in which each makes only those voluntary agreements about allocation and distribution that he is willing to make?), it is none the less true. As a consideration of the examples used in the economic literature shows, what is envisaged is a situation in which each is free to act bounded only by existing, specific, contractual agreements and the ability to buy what he wants. There is no reference to principles of altruism, communitarian concerns, 'neighborliness,' or the like. It is not that such things are disapproved of, of course; it is just that, except as prudent steps toward maximizing an individual's own satisfactions, they do not enter into the designs for the ideal property rights structure. What this means is that this purely economic argument views with equanimity any obnoxious use an owner might make of a piece of property as long as it does not violate a contract and as long as those harmed by it are (rationally) unwilling to pay the offender enough to make it worth his or her while to desist.[22] While such robust individualism is appealing to some, it is by no means appealing to all. Most people, I suspect, think that motives count, and that in so far as possible the system of property rights should be designed to discourage malicious or casual disregard of other people's welfare even when it is in one's economic interest to do so. Similarly for communitarian concerns: without some legal insulation from whatever external disutilities others can create, individuals who do not keep enough 'dollar votes' to buy off those others will be at a disadvantage. They will thus be forced to be *only* rational self-maximizers. Generosity to others, at least in so far as it in any way costs one dollar votes, will have negative survival value. To reply by saying that if people really believe these virtues of generosity and kind motives are important, then they will in effect have cash value and work to one's advantage, is to miss the point. Unless one can *count* on reciprocity for one's good neighborliness — not just from 'most people' but from all the ones whose choices can actually create disutilities for one — then self-protective dollar votes will have to be kept. And generosity will be expensive indeed.

In addition to this difficulty, there is a serious problem with the notion of measuring efficiency and justice by dollar votes. How are such votes to be distributed in the ideal model? Even if one envisages an absolutely equal initial distribution, it is clear that the idealized free market model is not designed to preserve equality. It would be utterly trivial if it did, for it would define economic stasis, not a dynamic system. In any plausible dynamic model, the pull to move away from equality will be continuous. Beyond subsistence needs, people have very different wants; accidents and inventions produce new wealth for some; transactions from which some are net gainers and others net losers (for example, in terms of holdings of productive resources) are inevitable. But once inequality enters, a serious problem is created for the model. Those with more votes will obviously be able to force or prevent changes to the disadvantage of others. For example, given the declining marginal utility of each dollar beyond a certain point (i.e. dollar X being 'worth more' to a person than dollar X+1 than dollar X+2, etc.), when the relatively poor create disutilities for their relatively rich neighbors, it will cost the rich less to 'buy off' the disutility than it would cost the poor to do the same. This is so because the dollar votes required to compensate the poor person who is paid to refrain from causing the disutility 'mean less' to the rich than the poor. Thus the rich can avoid externalities that the poor cannot, and if the avoidance of these externalities has positive consequences for the production of goods, the initial advantage to the rich snowballs. Even more obviously, in competition for the same good, the rich will outbid the poor; and when selling the same good, will underbid the poor. This tendency will, if it goes far enough, be destructive of the fundamental notions of the model. That is, it will move things away from perfect competition and voluntary exchanges. So in any attempt to realize the model in the world, devices designed to limit this tendency will have to be installed. Further, of course, people in the real market are not always able to assess what is in their rational self-interest and then to act on it. Even not counting children, the mentally handicapped and so forth, abilities to calculate advantages differ. And transaction costs can be substantial. So devices to correct for these things will also have to be developed. It is not at all obvious that the necessity for these devices will contribute to the justification of certain sorts of property rights. It seems much more likely that it will justify severe limitations on specific property rights.

A final difficulty with this form of economic argument is premise (5), which asserts that any change in allocation or distribution which does not move things toward the economic ideal is unjustified. This is a direct challenge to pluralists — those who will argue that there are important social goals which must be balanced against whatever legitimacy these economic ones have.[23] This premise is, after all, remarkably non-historical in character. It and the conclusion, (6), disregard entirely the issue of a person's pre-existing *title* to have things remain unchanged.

The argument apparently authorizes any change (forced by government? one's neighbors?) which approximates what would happen under 'ideal' economic circumstances. But if property *rights* are to mean anything, surely they must mean that one can refuse to use the property to approximate the ideal of everyone's rational self-maximization. The upshot is that this form of economic utility argument, while ostensibly designed to secure a sweeping variety of full ownership property rights, seems to justify breathtaking cancellations of those rights whenever it would serve to move things in the direction of the ideal model.

PARTICULAR JUSTIFICATION

This is perhaps even more obvious when one imagines the application of economic efficiency arguments to the adjudication of particular conflicts over who should have what rights. Here our concern for bringing in existing rights to block changes which are unwanted by those who lose from them is very strong — *even when adequate compensation is offered*. Further, there are good grounds for the suspicion that compensation will in fact be offered selectively — on behalf of a quite different notion of economic efficiency: that of maximizing the grand total of marketable satisfactions *per se*.[24] Economic utility arguments at this level are not used to establish rights; they are used to override them.

6 The Argument from Political Liberty *

The argument
One may argue in the following way for property rights as a consequence of liberty.

(1) It is a fact that human beings will try to acquire things, control them, exclude others from their use, modify them, and use them as wealth.

(2) The effective prohibition of such activities — i.e. the elimination of private property altogether — would require a comprehensive and continuous abridgment of people's liberty which (even if it were possible to carry out) is at best unjustifiable and at worst flatly prohibited by the existence of political liberties to which people are entitled, morally.

(3) The regulation of acquisitive activities, by what amounts to a system of property rights, is likewise required to preserve liberties to which people are entitled.

(4) Therefore, property rights are justifiable.

This is, of course, only a *general* justification, for it does not specify what sorts of things people are entitled to own, and what sorts of property rights they are entitled to have in those things. And it makes property a derivative, rather than a fundamental, right; it assumes the prior justification of an extensive system of political liberty.

The soundness of the argument
Premise (2) is clearly the crucial one. The first premise merely asserts that people will try to do what the utility argument says they need to

---

* Throughout this chapter, the term 'political' is used as a modifier for 'liberty' in the same way it is used in the phrase 'political science.' I do not, for example, mean to distinguish political from religious liberties or political from civil liberties. All liberties guaranteed by the state are, in this usage, political liberties.

do. The connection is a contingent one, however, so the soundness of the argument is restricted to societies in which people do, persistently, try to satisfy these needs. But this is not a restriction which has much practical signficance.

Premise (3) is equally uncontroversial. The liberty to acquire things is surely not the only liberty to which people are entitled. (Or less forcefully, *if* it can be shown that they are entitled to the liberty to acquire, surely it can be shown that they are also entitled to the liberty to live free from malicious harms inflicted by others.) Since it is clear that unregulated liberties to acquire would result in the unjustifiable abridgment of some people's liberties to live or maintain their health, and since the liberty to live or maintain one's health is surely a liberty equal to or greater in importance than the liberty to acquire, some regulation of the liberty to acquire is called for.

So premise (2) is the crux of the matter. One must show that people are entitled to a system of political liberty strong enough to include the liberty to acquire property rights and then show that the complete prohibition of such a liberty to acquire property would be an unjustifiable abridgment of political liberties whose existence is uncontested. I cannot provide a thoroughgoing defense of political liberty here, but I shall do enough to show that this argument for property rights is sound, assuming an amount of political liberty which is plausible in terms of a standard justificatory strategy. First, some preliminaries.

MATERIAL AND FORMAL LIBERTY

An important distinction in any discussion of liberty is the difference between what might be called material or actual liberty and formal liberty. I am formally at liberty to fly to New Haven by flapping my arms. That is, no one has any claim rights against me which prohibit it. But the liberty is purely formal — consisting only of the fact that the proposition 'I am at liberty to fly to New Haven by flapping my arms' is true. I cannot actually *do* so. Material or actual liberties are things I can actually do if I choose to. Some things I am at liberty *materially* to do, I do not have the formal (moral) liberty to do — i.e. the proposition that I am morally at liberty to do them is not true (cannot be justified). Formal liberties are thus of different sorts: I have the *logical* formal liberty to do whatever is non-contradictory, the *legal* formal liberty to do whatever the law allows, and the *moral* formal liberty to do whatever morality allows.

NATURAL AND INSTITUTIONAL LIBERTY

Liberties whose existence is not dependent on the existence of conventions or social institutions may be called natural liberties. In a Hobbesian state of nature each person has complete (logical, moral, and legal) natural liberty – in the sense of formal liberty. That is, no one has claim rights against anyone else for anything. Once various social institutions emerge, institutional liberties can also emerge. (See the discussion of liberty rights above, pp 12-13.)

FEATURES OF THE SYSTEM OF POLITICAL LIBERTY

Any system of political liberty strong enough to provide a general justification of property will have to have the following features:

First, it will have to distinguish political liberty from material liberty. That is, having the liberty to do something must be more than having the sheer physical or political ability to work one's will on others or things. There is, after all, nothing *prima facie* wrong with an act just because it restricts someone's power to do something. And the argument assumes that the restriction of a liberty is *at least* a *prima facie* wrong. (Else why be concerned to prohibit its restriction in this case?) So political liberties must be *rights* – at least Hohfeldian liberty rights, which entail the *absence* of claim rights in others that one *not* do or have the thing in question.

Second, to the extent that an account of political liberty seeks to provide a general justification of property, it will have to be talking about material, *as well as purely formal*, liberty. Political liberty is more than mere power, but it is not less than that. A liberty which is purely formal (e.g. my right to build a spaceship capable of speeds exceeding the speed of light) is a trivial matter, morally. Its restriction or elimination would have no practical consequences. Only in so far as my actual ability to do something (now or in the future) is hampered has my political liberty been infringed.

Third, since the existence of any material liberty at all (except the liberty to die) requires one's continued existence (for long enough to exercise the liberty), any system of political liberties strong enough to justify property rights must at least include the right to survive that long by one's own efforts. This means, in effect, that others must not have claim rights which destroy or restrict one's material liberty to survive by one's own efforts.

These three (minimal) features of any system of political liberty adequate to provide a general justification for property produce significant restrictions on what can legitimately be owned – and in what ways it can be owned. Wherever a resource necessary for survival is scarce, or non-renewable, or exhaustible by appropriation or misuse, unrestricted ownership will not be compatible with the general justification of property (from liberty). Further, wherever a thing can be used to interfere with another's liberty to survive, ownership rights will have to be restricted — specifically, use rights and management rights. More extensive systems of liberty — for example, ones which guarantee all or some the right to some degree of personal fulfillment or self-realization — will place even further restrictions on ownership.

THE JUSTIFICATION OF A SYSTEM OF POLITICAL LIBERTY

Political liberty is typically justified by appeal to the (rebuttable) presumption that it is wrong for one person to interfere with what another is doing. How that presumption is justified and how one gets from it to the existence of claim rights to political liberty is illuminating.

The justification usually begins by noting that in the absence of any semblance of a moral or political order, people are at liberty to do whatever they can do. No one has (claim) rights against another, and the absence of such rights in others is the existence of unrestricted liberty in each. The extent of one's liberty is the extent of what one can do (not what one wants to do or needs to do), and in this respect, people differ widely, depending on their physical and intellectual prowess, determination, courage, squeamishness, and so on. There is no 'material' equality of liberty, then, in a state of nature. But there is 'formal' equality, in the sense that the proposition 'People are at liberty to do what they can do' is equally true for each person. (And as Hobbes points out, the fact that the weak can kill the strong by stealth, take from them by deceit, and otherwise stay out of their way, produces a surprising approximation of material equality as well.)

The moral question, of course, is this: Among the things people are at liberty to do to each other, which ones ought they to do, and which ones ought they not to do? Answers come from a variety of lines of argument (e.g. various versions of utilitarianism), but the prospect of generating some moral rules out of the purely formal aspects of the situation has been a persistent fascination. (By 'purely formal aspects' I mean those which are independent of the [contingent] desires, needs, or abilities of people in a state of nature. The formal equality of liberty is one such aspect. Any desires or needs or abilities which are necessarily present in each person in a state of nature would be other formal aspects.) The requirements of rationality are presupposed — that is, the canons of deductive validity and inductive 'soundness' — not because people in a state of nature are necessarily rational, but because the moral question (as addressed to philosophers) asks for answers which can be rationally justified.

The problem is thus to see what ordering, if any, of the material liberties people have in the state of nature is required by reason. Here the formal equality of liberty and the canon of self-consistency have been thought to combine to produce important results.

Consider: the point of the state-of-nature thought-experiment is to define the (imaginary) situation prior to any human interactions and to see what picture of rationally *justifiable* interactions can be built up from it. The situation prior to any human interactions includes formal equality of the liberty of each — that is, the liberty of each to do what he or she can in fact do. Any changes in that situation due to subsequent human interactions require justification — that is, they are precisely the sort of things the philosopher is asked to provide a reasoned justification for. So unless a change can be justified, the formal equality of liberty must be preserved.

Now it is clear that in human interactions, the only way the truth of the proposition 'Each is at liberty to do what he or she can do' can be preserved is if the actions of each do not infringe the material liberty of others. To the extent that my acts limit you in the exercise of your abilities to act, you are not at liberty to do what you can do. Thus, to preserve the formal equality of liberty, others must not act so as to limit my material liberty, and I must not act so as to limit theirs. Put more formally:

(1) Each person, in a state of nature, is at liberty to do what he or she can do — i.e. has formal equality of liberty and material liberty to the extent defined by his or her abilities.

(2) Any change, due to human interactions, in the range of persons for which (1) is true, requires justification.

(3) Anyone who exercises his or her liberty in a way which limits another's exercise of liberty changes (1) — so far without justification.

(4) To refrain from exercising (some part of) one's material liberty does not represent a change in (1).

(5) For (1) to remain unchanged (i.e. to remain true for all) in the context of human interactions, each must refrain from acting in ways which limit the exercise of other's (material) liberty.

(6) Therefore, unless a change in the system of material liberties is specifically justifiable, each person must refrain from interfering with the material liberty of others. (The 'must' here is a moral one, meaning that to do otherwise is to act unjustifiably.)

This much is sound. The next step is to get from (6) to the assertion that people have *claim rights* to liberty. Here a number of approaches are available, from straight utility arguments to various contractarian arguments, the most potent of which is undoubtedly Rawls's.[1] It seems clear that where a presumption against interference with material liberty exists, one can justify shoring up that presumption with the relevant claim rights and duties. One would merely have to establish the following premises:

(7) If people do not act so as to preserve (1), or they are not likely to so act, it is reasonable — in the absence of countervailing reasons to the contrary — to require them to so act, in the sense that, should they not, it would be justifiable to use coercive measures to extract either the act or compensation in lieu of it.

(8) To be so required to act is to have a duty to so act.

(9) If each has a duty not to limit the liberty of others, then each has a right to material liberty only if it is compatible with the material liberty of others.

And (7) is the crux of the matter, for (8) and (9) are true by definition.

The reasonability of requiring people — in the sense specified in premise (7) — not to interfere unjustifiably with others' material liberty cannot seriously be questioned, I think. Both utilitarian and hypothetical-contractarian theories have successfully argued for equivalent principles.[2] And the connecting link between moral liberties and a system of political liberty is simply an argument to the effect that certain requirements (of morality) are properly incorporated into a legal system and enforced as legal rights. Which requirements these are is a somewhat controversial matter, but there is agreement from all but the anarchists that some rights should be legally enforced,[3] and agreement that these rights are at least those necessary to guarantee survival by one's own efforts. Thus the argument from the notion of material liberty forms the basis for the argument (for property) from political liberty.

The crucial remaining question is: *What conditions are sufficient to defeat the non-interference presumption (and thus invalidate the corresponding claim rights)?* Here the battle lines between utilitarians and libertarians are drawn. And it is clear that in current practice, the utilitarians win more skirmishes than they lose.[4] The justification of specific property rights will need clear guidance on this issue. But it is enough for present purposes to have established the soundness of the presumption against interference with material liberty, the consequent soundness of the corresponding claim rights, and the way in which these claim rights form the basis for a general justification of property rights.

7 Considerations of Moral Character

It has occasionally been held that property should belong to the property-worthy. 'Property-worthy' has meant, variously, 'one who will use property to good effect,' 'one who will manage property well,' or just 'one who is virtuous.' In each case the asserted ground for title to property rights is different, but in each case it is related to considerations of the moral character of the property-holder. Further, these arguments all assume that a general justification of property rights has been given, that it includes the sort of considerations brought forward in the general form of the utility argument, and that the specific sorts of property rights at stake have been determined. The arguments here address themselves solely to questions of who ought to have the specified rights.

People who will use property to good effect
This argument is that ownership of some kinds of things is 'lost' on some people — meaning that the values they derive from it, as opposed to the values others could derive from it, are shamefully small. The objection is often made by saying that a thing is 'too good' for its owner. It arises frequently in the case of art, when people are unhappy about the fact that others with money but no sensitivity or concern for works can buy them merely as investments. No matter how much the ownership of such property is due to labor, no matter how useful it is (for the artist, for the art world, for the society at large), the force of this objection is felt. The line of argument which produces it goes something like this:

(1) The general justification for acquiring property rights in a thing is at least in part to secure the carrying out of purposes for or with the thing.

81

(2) It is wasteful for things not to be well used — that is, for them not to be employed to the greatest advantage.

(3) Waste is morally objectionable in the case of scarce goods.

(4) Some people are better able to use certain goods to the greatest advantage than others.

(5) Thus, if goods can justifiably be owned by individuals at all, those goods (at least if they are scarce) ought to be owned by the people who can and will use them to greatest advantage.

This argument may include need as one of several principles for finding out who can use a thing to greatest advantage, but it is not *based* on need in the way the utility argument is. Here need is linked to the notion of property-worthiness by way of the 'greatest use' and 'prohibition of waste' principles. The argument is clearly elitist in some applications, but sweeping and radical in nearly all its applications. It secures the rights of the initiated to the esoteric — whether in art or in agriculture — but also secures a distribution according to greatest benefit among the initiated. Since some 'initiations' are nearly universal (e.g. eating), the argument would appear to support a rather egalitarian distribution of property in the goods necessary to life. (I say 'rather' egalitarian because it does not support property rights for those who are so helpless as to be unable to use even the necessities to their advantage.)

The weaknesses in the argument lie in the second and third premises. If the prohibition of waste is taken to be a *requirement* of all ownership, so that to show that something is not being used to greatest advantage simply eliminates or overrides any other justifications to title, then a very tenuous claim has been made. I know of no way to justify it. If, however, the claim is merely that waste is an objection which can sometimes invalidate other justifications to title, then the tenor of the argument is significantly changed. The conclusion will hold only in so far as no competing justifications for property rights produce a different conclusion. The argument is at most one of a larger set of considerations justifying property rights.

There is another difficulty with premise (2), however, which weakens the argument still further. This is the ambiguity of the phrases 'well used' and 'greatest advantage.' Are these phrases to be taken to refer to the greatest *social* (or general) advantage? Or merely the greatest advantage to the individual who owns the thing? The former requirement is certainly plausible where the thing owned is something which others *need* to have well used, and which is unavailable to them otherwise. But this interpretation turns the argument into a version of the argument from utility, and one which leads in the direction of prohibiting private ownership in the cases mentioned rather than merely requiring private owners to use their property for the good of all. At least, to retain private ownership, one would have to show that it was more likely to yield the needed general good than public ownership.

To keep the argument distinct from the utility argument, then, it seems necessary to assume that the phrases 'well used' and 'greatest advantage' in premise (2) refer to the advantages obtained from ownership by the individual owner. The conclusion, which we have already noted is only one of several competing lines of argument, is now quite vulnerable to considerations of utility, when those conflict with individual advantage. Still, with all its qualifications, it is an interesting and valid line of argument.

People who will manage property well

The argument here is schematically similar to the previous one – with the same difficulties and eventual highly qualified conclusion. The emphasis is somewhat different, focusing as the word 'manage' indicates, on the owner's ability to run things rather than wring personal advantage from them. In outline, the argument goes like this:

(1) The general justification for acquiring property rights in a thing is at least in part to secure the success of the carrying out of purposes for or with the thing.

(2) It is wasteful for things not to be well used – that is, for them not to be employed to the greatest advantage.

(3) Waste is morally objectionable in the case of scarce goods.

(4) Some people are better able to manage certain goods to the greatest advantage than others, and where good management is necessary to good use, it follows that:

(5) If goods can justifiably be owned by individuals at all, those goods (at least if they are scarce) ought to be owned by the people who can and will manage them to greatest advantage.

What this version of the argument shows is the (occasional) necessity for distinguishing between use rights and management rights with respect to ownership. Clearly, for a given thing X, and two individuals A and B, if A can manage X but not use it to advantage, and B can use X but not manage it, then the ownership rights to X ought to be divided (assuming there is no countervailing argument to the contrary).

The virtuous

We sometimes think that good people deserve to get and keep good things – merely from the fact that they (the people) are good. More often, we object when the wicked have good things (no matter how honestly acquired). There is even a strand (not a mjaor one, to be sure) in Christian theology to the effect that property properly belongs to the righteous.[1] It seems initially unlikely that anything very significant for the theory of property rights can be built on these foundations, but they yield some surprises.

Consider: even if it is true that what is earned is deserved, it does not follow that what is unearned is undeserved. Or rather, perhaps one should say that good character 'earns' things as much as labor does. Specifically, good fortune (unearned by labor) is none the less said to be deserved when it falls to the virtuous, and undeserved when it falls to the wicked. We all share Job's sense of injustice when the wicked prosper and the good are struck down by calamity after calamity. It is not that the wicked do not deserve the fruits of their (honorable) labor. And it is not that the virtuous deserve something for nothing. It is rather the recognition that:

(1) Some goods are the product (partly or wholly) of events which have nothing to do with one's intelligence, labor, or moral character. They come by chance, or from the caprice of other agents.

(2) Such goods (hereafter: good fortune) play a significant role in determining people's access to (the means to) well-being, happiness — and in competitive situations, to competitive advantage. Similarly, bad fortune plays a significant role in determining the opposite.

(3) Good fortune is in no way deserved by the wicked, but it is in one way deserved by the virtuous (whatever one's definition of virtue is). The virtuous deserve good fortune in the same way they deserve respect, admiration, and gratitude; it is appropriate; it is fitting; it is an event logically and psychologically compatible with good conduct and character.

(4) Thus, to the extent that good fortune can be controlled (e.g. by distributive measures after the fact), it should go only to the virtuous.

There are two problems with this argument, I think. The first is the interpretation of 'deserve' in premise (3); and the second is the assumption that goods should go only to those who deserve them. (The first two premises seem to me to be clearly true.)

'Deserve' is apparently used in premise (3) to include only 'what one has earned with labor' and 'what is logically and psychologically compatible with one's conduct and character.' Problems with the former sense have been discussed in the chapter on the labor theory. But granting this as a legitimate usage of 'deserve,' what about the other usage — the one on which the whole argument hinges? Does it really clarify matters to say that one deserves something in the sense that having it is logically and psychologically compatible with one's conduct and character? I think it does. The psychological compatibility spoken of is, after all, only a reiteration of the facts about our responses to the distribution of good fortune which began the whole argument. We just *do* react adversely to goods falling by fortune to the wicked; and we just *do* react with satisfaction (at least when problems of envy are removed) to such goods falling to the virtuous. The 'logical compatibility' spoken of is simply that to the extent that a good is a 'reward' or 'desert,' it must be a reward or desert for something, and for something *good*. It would make nonsense of the concept of desert to speak (unless ironically or figuratively) of a good as one's desert for doing or being evil.

But there is another problem of interpretation which is not as easily resolved. Earlier in this chapter, two notions of property-worthiness were discussed which are apparently ignored by this argument. A person who will use or manage something to greatest advantage can legitimately be said to deserve it. Yet this may have nothing to do with our overall judgment of the person's moral character. So it seems possible, after all, for a wicked person to deserve the products of good fortune — not in either of the senses of 'deserve' used in the argument, but in another, equally legitimate, sense. The argument must be modified to acknowledge the possibility of other forms of desert.

Similarly, it must acknowledge, I think, that desert is not the only principle by which the products of good fortune are (justly) distributed. Sometimes utility is rightly a factor. The amended argument will thus have to be something like this:

(1) Some goods are the product of (partly or wholly) events which have nothing to do with one's intelligence, labor, or moral character. They come by chance, or from the caprice of other agents.

(2) Such good fortune plays a significant role in determining people's access to (the means to) well-being, happiness — and in competitive situations, to competitive advantage. Similarly, bad fortune plays a significant role in determining the opposite.

(3)[1] Good fortune may not be deserved by the wicked, but it is always deserved by the virtuous in the sense of its being logically and psychologically compatible with their conduct and character.

(4)[1] Thus, to the extent that the products of good fortune (a) can be distributed; and (b) ought to be distributed only to those who deserve them; and (c) are not deserved by the wicked (or the morally 'neutral'), they ought to go only to the virtuous.

Translated into an argument for property rights, the conclusion asserts that (in the absence of countervailing arguments from other forms of desert or from utility) the portion of property acquired by means of good fortune should go to the virtuous. (This assumes that the property can justifiably be held by individuals and that the portion ascribable to good fortune is ascertainable and distributable. It also, of course, assumes that the virtuous can be identified.) Who among the virtuous should get what portion of the property is not specified. One assumes that, for divisible property, perhaps the presumption in favor of equal distribution would obtain, rebuttable by further discriminations with regard to desert, need, and utility. For non-divisible goods, the presumption most true to the spirit of the argument would assign priorities by degrees of desert (with some method for breaking ties), the priority assignments then being challengeable by utility considerations and so on.

Property as necessary for the development of moral character

In addition to the arguments based on property-worthiness, there is another issue raised by considerations of moral character. It is sometimes suggested that being an owner of things is a necessary condition for the development of some elements of virtuous character. Aristotle remarks, for example, that property-holding is necessary for developing self-control and liberality (generosity?).[2] But turning remarks like this into a sound argument for property rights is a difficult task. It is difficult because the argument will depend on contestable premises about what counts as an element of virtuous character, as well as contestable premises about human behavior.

Leaving such problems aside, however, it is difficult to see how owning things- is a necessary condition for the development of any possible element of virtue. If skills of various sorts are elements of virtue (skills of use or management, for example), they can be developed without owning property. The use of the things one needs to learn on (together with whatever instruction is available) is all that is required. If creativity of various sorts is an element of virtue, and if it requires the use of things or the consumption of raw materials for its development, then again it is hard to see why protected possession and the liberty to use and consume are not sufficient. The claim right to possession, let alone the rights to income, capital, and transmission, are irrelevant. The 'dispositional virtues' — e.g. temperance, self control, perseverance, generosity — can all be developed without private property. No doubt property can help, but one can teach a child generosity with reference to personal services as well as with reference to things owned. Likewise self control, temperance, and perseverance develop as much from dealing with promises, expectations, delays in gratification, and (property less) social interactions generally as they do from dealing with things one owns. In short, the argument appears to deserve its disuse.

8 Anti-Property Arguments

Opponents of property rights use two sorts of argument: refutations of arguments given in support of property; and 'positive' arguments designed to show that property rights (at least of some specified sorts) ought not to exist. The attempted refutations have been considered in the course of evaluating the arguments from first occupancy, labor, utility, and virtue. The 'positive' arguments against property rights, however, deserve separate attention.

They may be divided into four general types: arguments to the effect that property rights have an overall social disutility; arguments to the effect that the institution of property rights is self-defeating; arguments to the effect that private ownership produces vicious character traits (i.e., that its abolition is necessary to the development of moral character); and arguments to the effect that systems of property rights produce and perpetuate unjustifiable socio-economic inequality. (This argument from inequality is the most interesting, and probably the most potent of the four. I have put it last only for convenience of exposition.)

Social disutility

The utility argument for property rights asserts that people need to acquire, possess, use, and consume things — and that their need to do so can only be met through instituting a system of private ownership. Anti-property theorists do not accept those contentions, as I have already mentioned. But some of them also advance an argument, itself based on utility, which is designed to show that the institution of property rights has an overall social disutility — that is, that on balance it produces a net loss of good — no matter whether people need such rights or not. The outlines of this argument to disutility, as I shall call it, are as follows.

88

THE ARGUMENT

(1) Any system of property rights which permits private ownership (in the full, liberal sense) of land or the means of production which are scarce, or are non-renewable, or are capable of monopolization, inevitably produces inequality in wealth of a sort which increases over generations, hardens the social order into a class structure, and (a) yields an unjustifiable amount of poverty, and (b) yields an unjustifiable amount of social instability.

(2) It is not necessary to permit private ownership of the things mentioned above. That is, (a) private ownership of those things is not necessary for survival, a reasonable degree of happiness, or the full development of personality; and (b) prohibiting private ownership of those things is an enforceable policy.

(3) Whatever needs are satisfied by private ownership (in the full, liberal sense) of land or the means of production which are scarce, or are non-renewable, or are capable of monopolization are minor compared to the needs for social stability and the elimination of poverty.

(4) Since the social stability people need is impossible given a system which permits private ownership of those things (from (1) above), and since the need for such stability outweighs any needs people have for private ownership of those things (from (3) above), and granting that the prohibition of such ownership is possible (from (2) above), it follows that private ownership of those things ought not to be permitted.[1]

THE SOCIAL STABILITY PREMISE

The first premise of this argument is in part an assertion about matters of fact — facts about the social conditions which would result from full, liberal, private ownership of certain things. The assessment of its truth as a general proposition about social and economic phenomena is difficult because it is so general. It is certainly convincing as an assertion about how things often *have* turned out. One does not have to read much history to find property distributions cited as causes for abject poverty, wars, revolutions, and less massive sorts of instability.

But whether the institution of property rights (for the things specified) always must produce poverty and social instability just seems to me beyond anyone's power to determine. One can, after all, imagine circumstances in which it would *not*, and those circumstances are not all utopian fantasies. If, for example, certain changes in popular attitudes, values, and beliefs about competitiveness and justice in distribution were to take place — changes comparable in scope to those which have occurred gradually in Western democracies in the last two hundred years (e.g. on issues such as slavery, taxation, tort liability, the nature of the family) – then the outcome would be different. It does little good, in a discussion of how things *ought* to be, to argue that such possibilities are unlikely, or simply will not occur. The argument as stated requires proof of the inevitability of poverty and social instability. Any possibility that a system of private ownership (of the things at issue) would *not* produce these conditions means that this whole argument can be countered by property theorists.

Even so, the first premise can be recast to support an important and powerful argument. One may say that *whenever* a system of private ownership produces sufficient poverty or social instability (and supposing premises (2) and (3) to be sound), then the conclusion (4) follows. The revised premise preserves the rationale for the original disutility argument against property rights, and in view of the frequency with which systems of private ownership actually produce these situations, the revised argument remains a potent objection to such systems.

That is, it remains so, assuming that the other premises are sound and that some conceptual problems with all the premises can be resolved. The first premise, for example, makes the phrases 'unjustifiable amount of poverty' and 'unjustifiable amount of social instability' central to the whole argument. The meaning of those phrases needs to be carefully spelled out. Premise (2) relies on a notion of necessity which needs attention. And premise (3) presupposes that needs can be rank ordered as to importance.

CONCEPTUAL PROBLEMS WITH THE ARGUMENT

'Poverty' (the economic variety) is definable in various ways. It always involves the notion of a significant shortfall of goods relative to some standard, but the standard may plausibly be defined in a number of ways: (1) as the amount necessary for physical survival, (2) the amount necessary for the maintenance of physical health, (3) the amount necessary for a reasonably comfortable and secure existence in good health, (4) the amount necessary for the full development of personality, (5) the amount necessary for 'normal' self-realization (however defined), (6) the amount necessary for carrying out some specified set of standard projects, or (7) some amount relative to what the wealthiest members of society have. The last defines poverty as relative deprivation, and given the impact such deprivation can have on a social order, might well be chosen for the disutility argument. The next to last – (6) – does not really stand on its own, but is introduced to operationalize one of the other standards. The first seems too severe; it is rather an

understatement to describe the situation in which a person does not have enough to sustain life as poverty. The maintenance of physical health — (2) — and the maintenance of a reasonably comfortable and secure existence — (3) — are better standards. But they miss some important things which (4) and (5) try to capture. If there are enough goods to permit a distribution which gives everyone the means for self-realization (however defined), or just the full development of persona lity,[2] and if some people have in fact achieved such affluence, then economic circumstances falling significantly short of those levels can plausibly be described as poverty. (If no one has ever achieved such affluence, however, there is little plausibility in describing the short-fall as poverty. My authority for this remark — and thus its sole signifi-cance — is simply an appreciation of common usage.)

In summary, then, conditions in which people are deprived of the means to maintain physical health, or of the means to secure a reason-ably comfortable existence, are clearly describable as poverty. Beyond that, the standards seem tied to some notion of relative deprivation. The argument to disutility may go through (or not go through) with any of several definitions of poverty.

But what is an 'unjustifiable amount' of poverty? Since this is a utility argument, the definition will not be tied directly to personal desert. (These considerations are reserved for the arguments from virtue and from inequality, below.) Rather, an 'unjustifiable amount' of poverty will be defined in terms of economic efficiency (see the relevant discussion in chapter 5). Any amount of poverty (i.e. number of people in a condition of poverty) greater than that permissible for economic efficiency is unjustifiable.

Social instability. Likewise, the definition of 'social instability' and the principle which determines its justifiable amounts has a great deal to do with the soundness of the first premise. Social instability means one thing to the timid, quite another to the reckless. It may occur in forms as non-violent as the general disregard of a corrupt legal system, in forms as pervasive as the sort of political tensions which make effective government impossible, and in forms as intense and bloody as violent revolution. What forms of instability are to count for the purposes of the disutilty argument, and how much of each is justifiable?

The answer to these questions is, in principle, rather straightforward. All forms of social instability which (considered alone) produce a net loss of good (however defined) count for the purposes of the disutility argument, and any amount which, *all things considered*, represents a net loss of good is an unjustifiable amount. To explain: suppose perfect social stability is defined as the state of affairs in which everyone does exactly what he or she ought to do – in the broadest sense of ought, a sense which includes not only obligation but the maximization of good and the exemplification of virtuous character as well. (Such perfection is mercifully only a definitional starting point.) Deviations from perfect social stability do not all (considered separately) produce a net loss of good. Some personal shortcomings may be harmless, for example. And failure to meet an obligation – say to meet a friend at 4 p.m. at a certain street – may turn out all right if the friend also fails to be there. Other deviations which, considered alone, produce a net loss of good may none the less prevent larger losses. If the gas line at that street explodes at one minute past 4, it is a good thing neither party was there.

In situations of *im*perfect social stability, some sorts of conduct which would be wrong in perfectly stable conditions are none the less required as a way of improving the imperfect situation. For example, in a case where the sacrifice of some particular good is required for the health or safety of all, but crucial people will not do what they ought – i.e. sacrifice those goods – coercion may be necessary. Such coercion, in an *im*perfectly stable situation, may be what people ought to do, even though it would be wrong in an ideal or perfect set of circumstances.

Both the utility and disutility arguments use lines drawn from the sort of general considerations just introduced. Assuming an imperfectly stable social order, it is possible to argue plausibly both that a system of property rights *reduces* the instability (though it may have elements which are themselves incompatible with perfect social stability) and that a system of property rights *increases* the instability (though prohibiting private ownership may have elements which are incompatible with perfect social stability). Premise (3) of the disutility argument addresses itself to precisely this issue, and though the battle over its soundness is typically fought about forms of social instability such as class warfare (as suggested by the wording of premise (1)), those extremes are only special cases of the general line of argument.

Necessity and need. The remaining conceptual problems with the disutility argument concern the notion of necessity introduced in premise (2), and the presupposition in premise (3) that needs can be rank ordered. About the latter, enough has been written by utilitarians to show that there is no problem here if rank ordering is all that is needed (and it is in this case). The problems come in trying to construct scales which specify either equality of intervals or equality of ratios – the so-called cardinality problem.[3]

The notion of necessity used in premise (2) may require a few words of explanation, however. The premise asserts that permitting private ownership (of the specified things) is not necessary for the satisfaction of the needs mentioned in the utility argument for property rights. That is, that it is not necessary for physical survival, a reasonable degree of happiness, or the full development of personality. So far the premise is simply a denial of the corresponding one in the utility argument. Premise (2) goes further, however, and asserts that the prohibition of (full) private ownership in land or the means of production which are scarce, are non-renewable or are capable of monopolization is an enforceable policy. This is done to fend off the objection that, like the Eighteenth Amendment, such prohibition would be unenforceable and therefore — whether one likes it or not — permitting private ownership in the things specified is necessary. This is a familiar enough notion not to need further elucidation here.

WHAT THE DISUTILITY ARGUMENT PROVES
The final question is, then, whether the premises of the disutility argument, as recast (in the case of (1)) and explicated, are sound or not. There is clearly no problem with the recast version of (1). It is no longer even a complete assertion. It merely begins the argument by saying that *whenever* a system of property rights yields unjustifiable amounts of poverty and social instability. . . (Some may think it too weak, since it refers only to property in land and some of the means of production. Why not extend it to private ownership *per se* — especially if it is already gutted of its assertions about the inevitability of the results of ownership? I have no objection to such an extension, but I think it is an empty gesture. That is, I cannot imagine a case in which the argument would go through for things which fall outside the categories now listed. Neither, I think, can the anti-property theorists who advance the argument, which is why they focus on the things specified in premise (1). It may be advisable to keep the possibility of such an extension in mind, however.)

Since (1) as revised really makes no assertion at all, the burden of the argument falls on (2) and (3). If they are sound, the conclusion (4) follows. And I can see no significant problem with (2), granted the efficient causes and time for making the changes in deep-seated attitudes the enforcement of such prohibitions might require. The real difficulties come with premise (3). Here one is required to weigh the net loss or gain from the prohibition of private ownership, and to do so one has to specify not only the social conditions which, together with private ownership, yield poverty and instability, but also the sorts and amounts of those things which outweigh any utility private ownership might have. The soundness of premise (3) thus cannot be assessed in the abstract, for in abstraction from a particular situation, the premise is only schematic. Once the necessary information is filled in, however (from a particular historical or hypothetical situation), the assessment should be no more difficult than routine utility ranking procedures legislators go through daily.

In summary, the disutility argument is the schema of a powerful objection to the existence of private ownership. As such it must be met by anyone defending a proposal for particular property rights. But because it is only schematic at the levels of general and specific justification, it can only be used to criticize particular proposals – and not to criticize the institution of property rights *per se*, or even certain species of those rights.

Self-defeatingness

It has often been remarked (and not by anti-property theorists alone) that any system of private ownership which attempts to guarantee to laborers the produce of their labor can become self-defeating when applied to land and means of production which are scarce, or are capable of monopolization. The following passage from an essay by Hastings Rashdall illustrates the point nicely.

> The best way of criticizing Locke's theory is to show that, when thought out, it contradicts itself. Let us suppose that ten men appropriate a desert island, divide it among themselves, and cultivate their respective shares. Each of them has ten sons, and having a taste for 'founding a family' leaves his share to the eldest. In the next generation there will be ten landlords and ninety landless men. These men have a sacred, natural right to the fruits of their labour: but how are they to exercise it? They will say to the elder brothers: 'We have a right to labour: let us work on your lands.' 'By all means,' the elder brothers will say, 'on condition of paying over to us all that the land produces over and above what will keep you and your families.' In that way the principle contradicts itself. The rights of property, supposed to be derived from a man's natural right to the fruits of his labour, involves the negation of that right in the non-inheritors of property. This is exactly what Karl Marx and the *a priori* socialists saw. They accepted Locke's own principle, and expressed it in the only logical form – 'the labourer has a right to *the whole* produce of his labour.' But this right is defeated by any appropriation of land and capital; therefore all land and capital, all the 'instruments of production' must be held in common. Thus the same principle

which was intended by Locke as the basis of a system of extreme
Individualism, has become the cornerstone of a system of
extreme and thoroughgoing Socialism.[4]

This is overstated, of course. It is not *any* appropriation of land, capital, and means of production which defeats the principle, but rather their *exhaustive* appropriation by some proper subset of the population. The argument applies only to private ownership of the specified goods; so it cannot be used to support total communism. But it is more than an attack on Locke's labor theory of acquisition. Any system — whether based on utility, first occupancy, labor, liberty, or virtue — which guarantees to people the products of their labors is vulnerable to this objection, *given certain additional circumstances.*

The additional circumstances required to make the self-defeatingness argument applicable are that the land or means of production actually *be* exhaustively appropriated by some subset of the population. To the extent that private ownership of these things is limited so that each unpropertied person retains the material liberty to appropriate (an equal share of) them, the argument has no force. Such limitation of ownership can occur, for example, when there is a frontier beyond which enough accessible land exists to satisfy the current population and when the society also has a population policy, as well as inheritance laws, designed to keep it that way. In such circumstances, one would still need to worry about 'virtual' or *de facto* monopolization — situations in which the prior acquisition of goods by one or a few can effectively block subsequent acquisition by others, even though there are unowned goods which are otherwise accessible. A further problem, in a modern industrial society, would be private ownership by corporations and foundations, which are exempt from the limiting influence of inheritance laws. Both problems are in principle manageable, however, even in a complex society where the quantity of unappropriated goods is small.

In sum, the self-defeatingness argument, like the disutility argument, stands as a source of objection to particular instances of the institution of private ownership — and then only to ownership in the full, liberal sense of the specified things. Further, of course, it only applies to systems which attempt to guarantee to persons the produce of their labor. More 'robust' systems, which make guarantees only that people are entitled to the produce of their labors *if* they can labor without trespassing on property previously acquired by others, escape this objection altogether.

Virtue

Plato is perhaps the first philosopher to have argued that private ownership has vicious effects on character. At a minimum, he thought that property interfered with the development of the traits necessary for the soldiers and rulers of the ideal state.[5] Some Christian theologians have taken passages from the Gospels and the book of Acts to mean that private ownership – or at least anything above that necessary for an ascetic existence – tends to block the achievement of whatever righteousness people can attain.[6] (Others simply argue that communal ownership is a New Testament command, whether private property has bad consequences for character or not. I do not refer to such positions here.)

This argument runs into exactly the sort of difficulty which defeats the corresponding argument *for* private ownership, the argument that property produces *good* moral character. The difficulty is that although one can easily imagine (even identify among one's acquaintances) private ownership as the cause of a certain character trait, one can just as easily imagine and find cases in which it is not. If acquisitions sometimes intensify acquisitiveness to the point of greed, they also can lead to generosity. If ownership can produce obsessive possessiveness, it can also produce a release from the constant worry some feel when property held in common is entrusted to them. I can see no possibility for a general argument here to the effect that property *always* produces more vicious than virtuous character traits. So the argument from virtue seems, like the other anti-property arguments, to be a schema for the critique of particular systems once they are spelled out, and not an injunction to systems of private ownership *per se.*

There is one area in which we typically think the effects of ownership must always be watched, however. That is the area in which governmental officials have an economic stake in the outcome of a case under their jurisdiction. To the extent that such conflicts of interest make impartial adjudication impossible, it may be necessary to hedge any system of private ownership with conflict of interest legislation. Similarly, to the extent that conflicts of interest destroy guarantees to consumers necessary for public safety, they may have to be further regulated. But these are merely probable outcomes for many sorts of systems in many sorts of circumstances. There is no more necessity here – and thus no more possibility of general anti-property argument – than in the other cases.

The perpetuation of inequality[7]

A final anti-property argument – and perhaps the most potent one of all — is one which has its source in a theme alluded to in both the social disutility and self-defeatingness arguments: namely that systems of private property rights can lock members of succeeding generations into positions of undeserved advantage and disadvantage. Significant socio-economic inequality defines significant differences in material (as opposed to formal) liberty — e.g. the liberty to travel, to get an education, to find rewarding employment. And it is correlated with differences in things as basic as health and life-expectancy.[8] Even if the original acquisitions were just, and even if the subsequent transfers were *procedurally* just, it cannot be just — so this argument goes — to permit the perpetuation of significant socio-economic inequality. The fact that some people did, and others did not, acquire property and pass it on to their heirs, is surely not sufficient justification for locking those heirs into positions of advantage or disadvantage.

Put more formally, the argument is this:

(1) Extensive systems of private property rights (even where rights of transmissibility are severely limited) tend to produce and perpetuate significant socio-economic inequality.

(2) Significant socio-economic inequality — quite apart from its propensity to create social instability — means that some members of society will be disadvantaged not only relative to others (e.g. with respect to material liberty), but absolutely (e.g. with respect to life-expectancy).

(3) No matter how just the original acquisitions were, and no matter how just (procedurally) the subsequent transfers were, those who (through no acts of their own) fall heir to the advantages or disadvantages mentioned in (2) cannot be said to deserve them.

(4) While undeserved advantages are unobjectionable if they do no harm to either the recipients or others, undeserved *dis*advantages ought to be prevented (or rectified) whenever possible.

(5) Some (significant) undeserved disadvantages are produced and perpetuated by the institution of property rights itself — regardless of limitations placed on transmissibility.

(6) Therefore, any institution of private property rights which is more extensive than the minimum required for social order is unjustifiable.

Matters of fact. I shall assume here that this argument has its facts straight. That is, I shall take it to be true that significant socio-economic inequality seriously disadvantages some people, and that an extensive system of private property rights — even if it drastically limits inheritance — produces and perpetuates some such disadvantages (e.g. the advantages of education accessible only to the children of high achievers

can be perpetuated in succeeding generations – to the relative disadvantage of others – regardless of inheritance laws).

Desert. Further, I shall assume that the ways in which the argument
makes use of the concept of desert are uncontroversial. Personal desert
claims must have a basis in personal conduct or character (see the
discussion of desert in chapter 4). What the argument asserts is simply
that advantages or disadvantages accrued through *no* act (or character
trait) of the recipient cannot have a basis upon which a claim that they
are deserved could be founded.

Necessary Evils. Moreover, the argument concedes that some significant inequalities produced by property rights may be uneliminable. For
instance, if the nuclear family is a justifiable social institution, and
laborers are to be compensated in proportion to their labor (points
granted by most), then it is inevitable – no matter how minimal the
system of property rights – that the parents' property will confer some
undeserved advantages or disadvantages on the children. While to some
this may provide grounds for abandoning the family as the basic social
unit, to most it only reveals that there are unavoidable bad consequences
associated with even the best social institutions.

But to acknowledge this is not to say that social institutions should
not be designed – in ways consistent with their justifiable functions –
to *minimize* bad consequences. And I take the relevant normative
premise in the argument to be uncontroversial: that undeserved disadvantages produced and perpetuated by private property rights ought
to be prevented or rectified whenever possible. (I take the 'whenever
possible' rider to mean 'whenever it is morally justifiable and humanly
possible to do so.')

Justice. The crucial weakness in the argument is its claim about
justice. It disregards or overrides claims based on justice in acquisition
and justice in transfer in favor of claims based on justice in distribution.
It asserts that, because some bad distributions are the inevitable result
of otherwise just acquisitions and transfers, those acquisitions and
transfers ought to be eliminated.

This is not a defensible position. What we have here are competing
claims for justice: one set for justice in acquisition and transfer (based,
for example, on arguments from labor, utility and liberty), and the
other set for justice in distribution (based on undeserved inequality).
The proper course is to deal with both sorts of claims in terms of the
rules for deciding conflicts among a plurality of arguments (see below,
chapter 9). But this anti-property argument is none the less a potent
source of limitations on systems of property rights – especially with
respect to inheritance.

9 The Justification of Property Rights

The positive results of the analysis so far may be summarized as follows: there are four independent and sound lines of general justification for private property – two from labor, one from utility (buttressed by two economic variants), and one from liberty. Because the arguments are independently sound, the general theory of property rights must make a place for them all (as well as for anti-property arguments), and because each can occasionally conflict with others in its application to problems of specific or particular justification, the general theory must *coordinate* them. Once coordinated into a coherent picture of general justification, any limitations they (or anti-property arguments) place on the justifiability of property rights must be observed at the levels of specific and particular justification – that is, those efforts must be *compatible* with the general justifications as coordinated. Some principles for compensation and taxation are built into the general justifications. In particular, the desert-labor argument entails penalties for the net losses caused by labor, the economic versions of the utility argument provide grounds for assessing both compensation and taxation, and the very concept of a right itself is such that any overriding of a right – whether justified or not – requires compensation. This last requirement places a significant burden on efforts to redefine rights after the fact (e.g. by passing laws which restrict or eliminate rights already held). Finally, within the constraints imposed by the four general justifications and the anti-property arguments, the labor and liberty arguments combine to produce a presumption in favor of allowing people to acquire as much property as they desire.

I want now to comment on each of these results in turn. The purpose is to bring the various elements of the analysis together at last, and to suggest some directions for the enterprises of specific and particular justification.

The plurality of general justifications

Traditional accounts — in some cases as reformulated here or by other writers — supply four sound lines of argument for a general justification of private property. Briefly, and somewhat formally put, they are as follows:

MILL'S ARGUMENT FROM LABOR

(1a) When the labor is beyond what is required, morally, that one do for others; when it produces something which would not have existed except for it; and when its product is something others lose nothing by being excluded from; then it is not wrong for producers to exclude others from the possession, use, management, and so forth of the fruits of their labors.

(1b) Whenever giving producers ownership rights in the fruits of their labors is a justifiable way of excluding others (under the conditions of (1a)), then such ownership rights are justifiable.

The limitations of this argument have been pointed out in detail (above, pp. 36-48). In particular, for competitive situations, the 'no loss' criterion is a very stringent one. And the fact that property rights (in so far as they involve claim rights for the holder) entail duties for others toward the owners, makes the no loss requirement, (1a), even harder to satisfy.

THE ARGUMENT FROM DESERT FOR LABOR

(2a) When it is beyond what morality requires them to do for others, people deserve some benefit for the value their (morally permissible) labor produces; conversely, they deserve some penalty for the disvalue their labor produces.

(2b) The benefits and penalties deserved are those proportional to the values and disvalues produced and those fitting for the type of labor done.

(2c) When, in terms of the purposes of the labor, nothing but property rights in the things produced can be considered a fitting benefit for the labor, and when the benefit provided by such rights is proportional to the value produced by the labor, the property rights are deserved.

When, in terms of the purposes of the labor, *either* property rights in the things produced *or* something else can be considered a fitting and proportional benefit, then either the property rights or one of the acceptable alternatives is deserved.

When, in terms of the purposes of the labor, property rights in the things produced cannot be considered a fitting benefit, or when the benefit of such rights is in excess of the values produced by the labor, the rights are not deserved.

(2d) Any diminution of value produced by the labor must be assessed against the laborer as a penalty deserved for the loss produced. (Penalties must be proportional to the loss produced, and a fitting remedy for that loss — fitting with respect to the purposes in terms of which it can be considered a loss.)

The soundness of (2a) is assumed — but not arbitrarily, for it meets the criteria for a primitive moral principle. The remaining steps are deduced from the concepts of desert, fittingness, benefit, and loss.

THE ARGUMENT FROM UTILITY

(3a) People need to acquire, possess, use, and consume some things in order to achieve (the means to) a reasonable degree of individual happiness and general welfare.

(3b) Insecurity in possession and use, and uncontrolled acquisition of the things people need (and want) makes achievement of (the means to) a reasonable degree of individual happiness and general welfare impossible (or very unlikely).

(3c) Security in possession and use and control of acquisition is thus necessary. But it is impossible unless enforced by an institution which amounts to the administration of a system of property rights.

(3d) Therefore, a system of property rights is necessary (or very nearly so) if people are to achieve (the means to) a reasonable degree of individual happiness and general welfare.

The crucial premise is clearly the first one. It may be argued for in the following way:

(i) People need to use and consume and possess some things merely for *survival* (food, shelter, etc.).

(ii) People are purposive; the satisfaction of the propensity to purposive activity (not necessarily any particular purpose) requires the consumption, possession, and use of some raw materials, and the expectation of continued use, etc.

(iii) Acquisition, possession, and use is necessary to the development of personality, self-esteem, and valued abilities, and the subsequent expression of personality, confirmation of self-esteem, and use of valued abilities.

(iv) Acquisition, possession, and use of things by one person can be a benefit to others as well as to the one who possesses, and occasionally the general welfare requires such acquisition and use by individuals.

The second and third premises may be extrapolated from the first — as in the traditional utility argument — or be argued for on independent grounds such as used by the general forms of economic utility arguments: cost-effective management of externalities and efficiency in resource allocation.

Utility thus provides a straightforward, clear, and convincing general justification for a system of property-right-making social institutions. Attempts to rebut its premises fail, in my judgment, and the *disutility* argument put forward by anti-property theorists has force only at the specific and particular levels of justification, not the general one.

THE ARGUMENT FROM POLITICAL LIBERTY

(4a) It is a fact that human beings will acquire things, try to control them, exclude others from their use, modify them, and use them as wealth.

(4b) The effective prohibition of such activities — i.e. the elimination of private property — would require a comprehensive and continuous abridgment of people's liberty which is at best unjustifiable and at worst prohibited by the existence of political liberties to which people are entitled, morally.

(4c) The regulation of acquisitive activities, by what amounts to a system of property rights, is likewise required to preserve political liberties.

(4d) Therefore, property rights are justifiable.

The crucial premise here is (4b), and the justifiability of a (minimal) system of political liberties is all that is required: a system in which liberties are at least Hohfeldian liberty rights, and in which the liberty to survive by one's own efforts is guaranteed materially as well as formally. This much can be accomplished with the familiar strategies of hypothetical-social-contract theorists or with a strategy based on the concept of natural liberty.

SPECIES CHARACTERISTICS: A PROGRAM FOR A FURTHER ARGUMENT

In addition to the traditional lines of argument, there is an additional possibility for buttressing arguments for property. It comes from the (possible) existence of certain characteristics of the human species. To the extent that the maintenance of individual distance, the acquisition of a territory, the establishment of dominance hierarchies, and the 'incorporation phenomenon' remarked on in the discussion of the labor theory are genetically determined characteristics of all normally formed human beings, they can function as presumptive support for traditional arguments, and thus for a system of property rights generally — perhaps even for a specific system. To explain:

The maintenance of personal or individual distance is a phenomenon often observed in animal behavior, and human behavior exhibits similar phenomena. A person will 'set boundaries' in nonintimate encounters, such that, when others inadvertently cross them, the person will draw away, trying to restore the 'proper' distance. And it may be that different distances are set for different purposes, so that people distributing themselves for conversation will tend to keep distances of x to y feet (variance due to differences in socialization), and people distributing themselves for the building of houses will tend to keep distances of (say) x_1 to y_1 feet. There is apparently some evidence from animal studies to suggest that territoriality becomes important when space is scarce enough so that the maintenance of individual distance is a difficult matter, and when it is so difficult as to require full-fledged social cooperation, dominance hierarchies tend to emerge as well.[1]

Now, if there are genetically based tendencies in humans toward the maintenance of individual distance, the acquisition of territory and the establishment of dominance relations, and if the things people produce with their labor or otherwise acquire tend to be psychologically 'appropriated' or 'incorporated' in the sense that one's concerns for one's person now extend to these things as well, then I think it is easy to see that the idea of ownership would have a (genetically based) 'appeal.' That is, one would expect normally formed humans to have an 'approval affect' toward ownership of the things they produce by their labor, and of the things necessary for the maintenance of personal distance. *Unless some reason can be given for concluding that this approval affect should not be followed out* (i.e. by instituting a system of property rights), *then it is not unjustifiable to do so.*[2] One thus has an 'ultimate' justification for the root idea of the labor theory and premises (3a) and (3b) above of the utility argument. Similar uses of species characteristics seem possible for the liberty argument.

At this stage, it would be presumptuous to call these considerations arguments. The empirical evidence is too scanty. But if what is now speculation should ever get sufficient empirical confirmation and elaboration, then moral arguments of the form I have described will be very important. Until that time, however, one has to make do with less thoroughgoing arguments.

The coordination problem

In principle it is possible for conflicts to arise if one general justification (say, from liberty) *requires* a certain sort of property right which another general justification (say, from utility) prohibits. (One assumes that prohibitions and requirements dominate mere permissions, such that if one general justification permits a certain property right, but a second general justification either prohibits or requires it, the second one is determinative.) Similarly, conflicts may arise between arguments *for* property rights (e.g. from liberty) and arguments *against* those rights (e.g. from inequality). These conflicts also form part of the coordination problem.

Now there are three ways conflicts between prohibitions and requirements can be decided rationally. One is by aggregation: if liberty and utility require x, but a labor argument prohibits it, then *unless there is some reason to weight the three elements of the conflict unequally*, two requirements outweigh one prohibition.

Some cases will not be decidable in this way, of course, e.g. cases in which the conflict is between equal numbers of prohibitions and restrictions. For them, one may be able to use a second method of resolution – that of weighting the elements of the conflict. In the case of one prohibition against one requirement, for example, only a rank ordering is required to decide the conflict.

But there is no reason to think, *a priori*, that all conflicts will be resolvable in either of these two ways – no reason to suppose that there could not just be deadlocks between conflicting prohibitions and requirements (of equal numbers or weight). In this third set of cases one must simply acknowledge that the outcome is a matter of indifference to reason and resolve the conflict arbitrarily – by the flip of a coin, for example.

Frequent conflicts will occur between liberty and utility, the desert form of the labor argument and utility, and all the pro-property arguments and the (anti-property) argument from inequality. I cannot provide anything more than a schema for the resolution of such conflicts here. And since the question of the priority of liberty over utility is a much discussed issue at the moment, it may be useful to frame the remainder of my remarks about the coordination problem in those terms. Making a case for the general priority of liberty over utility, or vice versa, would be a huge task. Even Rawls's principles refer only to 'basic' liberties – the sort which are constitutive of fundamental social institutions – and assert the priority of such liberties only for developed, reasonably affluent, societies.[3] But enough can be said here to provide reasonably explicit guidance for the enterprise of specific justification. And one can extrapolate principles from the remarks made on this problem to help in the resolution of other aspects of the coordination problem (e.g how to handle the competing claims of 'historical' and 'end-state' justice).

THE SEPARATENESS OF THE LIBERTY AND UTILITY ARGUMENTS

The argument from material liberty to political liberty establishes the independence of the argument (for property) from political liberty. That is, it is clear that political liberty has a source independent of considerations of utility − namely in the natural liberty of each person and the (rebuttable) presumption that interference with such liberty is wrong. There are also non-utilitarian arguments available for the step which authorizes the creation of a system of political liberties to reflect the presumption against interfering with the natural ones. Such political liberties may thus function as what Nozick calls 'side constraints' on moral goals rather than as a part of such goals.[4] But one still has no answer to the question of when, all things considered, such side constraints may justifiably be violated.

THE SELF-DEFEATINGNESS OF SOME VIOLATIONS

Just as the violation of some personal liberties cannot consistently be for that person's good (because they render a good life, or perhaps any life at all, impossible), so too the violation of some political liberties in the name of utility is self-defeating. It is clear that whenever the overriding of political liberties has this self-defeating consequence for the argument from utility, the liberty should be preserved. But this is no more than to say that there is disutility in violating the liberty in such cases. So it does not get one any closer to an account of when liberty should take priority over demonstrable utilities.

THE PRESUMPTIVELY EQUAL WEIGHT OF THE TWO ARGUMENTS

In fact, the soundest general course seems to me to be to treat liberty and utility *presumptively* as of equal weight, and to test that presumption (i.e. to try to rebut it) in specific cases. I say this because neither utilitarians nor liberty theorists have yet succeeded in producing a persuasive argument which would entail the general, across the board, dominance of one set of concerns over the other. That is, the theorists have not persuaded me directly, and have not persuaded enough of the knowledgeable readership to cause me to doubt my judgment. Discontent with a thoroughgoing utilitarian approach is widespread and seemingly permanent. Reluctance to subordinate utility to liberty across the board is just as widespread. So I see no rational alternative, at present, to treating the arguments from liberty and utility as of presumptively equal weight − at least in the case of the specific justification of property rights.

But how is the presumption to be tested in specific cases? What sorts of arguments can be given to justify weighting liberty more heavily than utility in some cases and utility more heavily than liberty in others? Here it helps to notice that there are three fundamental sets of moral concerns — ones related to the notion of value, ones related to the notion of duty or obligation, and ones related to the notion of moral character. Utility arguments are of the first sort — axiological concerns. Liberty arguments, when they are seen as constraints on social goods, are the second sort — deontological concerns. And arguments for the relative weight of liberty against utility can come from the third sort — characterological concerns. Whether the question is that of the nature of the virtuous person or that of the nature of the virtuous (i.e. ideal) society, to the extent that rational answers can be given to those questions such answers can help decide whether liberty or utility is to dominate a particular case. Which is the preferable social order: one which allows liberty X to remain intact despite its disutility? Or one which overrides the liberty in the interests of utility? Put so generally, such questions do not seem very promising as routes to the needed answers. But in specific sorts of situations, they may be answerable in a way which leaves no doubt about the relative weights to be given to utility and liberty. (Consider the standard example of scapegoating the innocent to secure social order. Here there are arguments to the effect that — with the possible exception of extreme and rare cases — social order which depends on such practices is not a worthy goal.)[5]

Conflicts between utility and the desert form of the argument from labor may be similarly analyzed (as may conflicts between liberty and labor arguments). The arguments are separate; the best course is to treat them as of presumptively equal weight; and the resolution of ties may be approached by bringing in additional considerations from moral character in the case of utility versus labor conflicts, and from axiology *and* moral character in the case of liberty versus labor conflicts. This procedure does not produce a tidy, hierarchically organized set of principles. But I see no reason to suppose, *a priori*, that moral principles are organizable in that way. The persistence of deep disagreements among reasonable, sophisticated theorists is evidence to the contrary. If the picture of the general justificatory framework for property rights is thus somewhat fuzzy, we may be at least partly consoled by a remark adapted from Wittgenstein: that a clear picture of a fuzzy thing is a fuzzy picture.

THE PRIORITIES OF THE LEGAL SYSTEM

It should be noted, however, that I have been speaking throughout of the question of *moral* priority — normative priority *per se* — and not of the more restricted issue of priority within some legal system. For a judge, the priority of liberty over utility *may* be decided by the fact that one has been given constitutional or statutory protection while the other has not. Or by some standard (legal) priority rule for ambiguous cases. But the moral question cannot be settled on such narrow grounds. The procedure above, messy as it is, seems the best way to settle it.

The compatibility requirement

It should be clear from the preceding analysis that the issue which now needs careful attention is specific justification — arguments to show what sorts of property rights people ought and ought not to have. As I remarked in chapter 1, this has always been the crux of the matter anyway, even though philosophers have typically found issues of general justification to be more diverting. If I have succeeded in my aim here, there has now been enough said on general justification for a while — enough to establish what the sound lines of general justification are; enough to define some important restrictions on any specific sort of property right which might be justified; and enough to give strong indications as to what sorts of property rights will be found to be justifiable. The first of these three results has just been summarized. I turn attention now to the other two.

The first thing of interest is what I have called the compatibility requirement. It is simply that specific sorts of property rights must be compatible with the available general justifications of property and with what is sound in the anti-property arguments. That is, they must not step over the restrictions imposed on all ownership by general justifications and anti-property arguments. Those restrictions, in summary, are the following: the (Millean) labor theory will not justify X's ownership of a thing if it constitutes a loss to any Y. The desert version of the labor theory will not justify property rights unless they are fitting and proportional benefits for the values produced — and then only when penalties for any disvalues produced are also assessed against the laborer. Further, and this is a very significant stricture, neither form of the labor theory is operative unless the labor at issue is other than what is morally required of the laborer. The argument from liberty requires that ownership not abridge the political liberties to which people are entitled. The argument from utility balances the disutilities caused by ownership against those caused by prohibiting ownership; it restricts property rights to those which have an overall net utility. And the (anti-property) argument from inequality is a source of restrictions on the right of transmissibility, as well as any other elements or varieties of ownership which perpetuate (unnecessarily) significant socio-economic disadvantages. In addition, of course, the other anti-property arguments (from social disutility, self-defeatingness and virtue) occasionally have some force.

When the relevant arguments have been coordinated for a particular range of cases – that is, when it has been decided whether they conflict and if so which arguments have priority – the dominant ones impose limits on specific justification. If the arguments do not conflict at all in a certain range of cases, then they all are operative, of presumptively equal weight, and the restrictions each imposes on specific justifications must be complied with. If utility conflicts with the liberty and labor arguments, and is subordinated to them for a certain range of cases, it becomes 'inoperative' there, and only the constraints imposed by liberty and labor arguments are relevant. (That is, they are the only relevant constraints drawn from the general justifications for property rights. There may be other constraints from other sources – constraints, for example, having to do with the perpetuation of inequality or the political realities of a given time and place.) Similarly, *mutatis mutandis*, for cases in which liberty and labor arguments are subordinated to utility.

(It should be remembered again that this discussion is framed in terms of moral argument. For legal argument, in cases where judicial duties are clear, the applicability of certain constraints – as well as the priority questions – may be settled by pre-existing sources of law.)

It will be useful to discuss in more detail some ranges of cases upon which the general justifications alone impose significant limits.

DUTIES TO OTHERS

If it can be established that we have positive duties of care toward others – that is, if beyond our negative duties not to do harm there are positive duties to do good – then the labor theory arguments are concomitantly restricted in their applicability. Each of the two sound labor arguments is limited to cases in which the labor at issue is other than what is morally required. So communitarians have an important opening wedge here against the 'as long as it does no harm' argument. If I have a *prior* moral duty to contribute positively to the welfare of my fellows, then until that duty is fulfilled (or its fulfillment is guaranteed in some way), I cannot work for myself, so to speak. That is, neither version of the labor theory will in that case provide a sound basis for claiming property rights.

But there are two interesting features of this limitation. First, the moral duty to contribute (positively) to the welfare of others must have *priority* over any moral requirements to work for one's own good.

That is, it is only *'prior'* moral duties which are at issue here now. It is reasonable to suppose that no positive duties to others could have priority over a requirement (if there is one) to do the (morally permissible) work necessary for one's own survival. And certainly many people would hold that one's positive duties to others cannot have priority over even one's *liberty right* to survive. That is, they would hold that there is no moral duty of (literal) self-sacrifice. But this is controversial, as is the further issue of whether 'figurative' self-sacrifice − in the form of inconvenience, expenditure of effort, etc. − is ever a moral duty in the absence of undertaking some special role (e.g. parent, physician) or making some special agreement. What is interesting is just that this important moral question is tied so directly to two important lines of argument for property rights.

The second interesting feature of this limitation on labor arguments is that some of my (positive) duties of care may be only toward a few (my family, say). Thus it may be that while the labor I perform to fulfill duties to my family does not justify the acquisition of property rights *against my family*, it may justify the acquisition of property rights *for my family* (me included) against everyone else. Thus one has a basis for holding that a child's entitlement to food, clothing, shelter, and the like is not at all weakened by the fact that the parents produced these things by their own labor.

EXHAUSTIBILITY

It is unlikely that any sort of property right could be justified whose implementation entails (or makes highly probable) the exhaustion of a significant resource by a subset of the total population. Such exhaustion would very likely constitute a loss to those left out, or be subject to prohibitive penalties for the losses caused, or amount to an interference with their liberty, or produce a net disutility, or perhaps all four. Either of the last two of these circumstances would be sufficient to prohibit it, in the absence of a conflicting requirement. And the exhaustion of a significant resource certainly would not be required by any of the lines of general justification (at least, I can think of no candidate for such a requirement).

Exhaustibility therefore will be a very large consideration in specific justifications. Goods such as space (in land, sea, or air) and matter can be exhausted simply by appropriation − that is, given the requisite system of property rights, a subset of the population can come to own all that is available.[6] Goods such as clean air and global water resources are exhaustible primarily by misuse rather than simple appropriation, but this is no less important for the theory of property rights. Uses which pollute the air or sea, for example, are likely to be prohibited by the general justifications of property, thus defining specific limitations on the use and management rights of owners. Goods such as fertile land, fresh water, fossil fuels, and wilderness areas are exhaustible either by appropriation or by misuse, and are also likely to be hedged with restrictions to prevent both.[7]

Technology and population size are important issues here. Things which were exhaustible only in principle several centuries ago are now in imminent danger of being exhausted. Specific justifications must change with such circumstances if nothing else (e.g. population policy) does; the justifiability of full, liberal ownership of land under the social conditions which existed in seventeenth-century North America does not guarantee that such property rights can be justified now. If they cannot, then the ownership rights in land must be redefined. And the question of injustice to current owners who possess the sort of title which is now unjustifiable, is not as serious as it might seem. In most cases, one probably will only need to change the rights of bequest and transfer so that only justifiable sorts of title may be passed on. This would leave the current owner's use, possessory, management, income, and security rights unchanged. And in situations so desperate that these rights must be redefined, compensation may be paid in lieu of honoring the right.

(It may be worth noting in passing that there *are* some goods which are not exhaustible by human agency — at least not with foreseeable technology. Sunlight and related radiation, magnetic energy, and electrical energy are all in this category. Materials used to convert these things to human use are exhaustible, of course. And sunlight can be blocked out. But the things themselves are not now vulnerable to exhaustion by appropriation or misuse.)

ACCUMULATION

Limitations on the sorts of property rights which can be justified arise when goods are exhaustible, then. But they can also come from the fact that accumulations which are prior to or much larger than the acquisitions of others can constitute a loss of competitive advantage for those others, or a restriction of their material liberty, or a serious enough, and widespread enough, frustration of human purposes to cause significant social instability.[8] This is the stuff of popular revolutions, and it is safe to say that none of the general justifications would license a system of property rights which had *all* these effects.

Clearly, however, conflicts between the prohibitions and restrictions of utility on the one hand and liberty on the other are likely. This is another juncture at which the weight of priority attached to liberty is a leading problem. If liberty has priority, in Rawls's sense, then no 'balancing' of utilities and liberties is possible; the demands of liberty must be satisfied first. If utility is given priority, then the situation is reversed. If liberties and utilities are weighted, however, balancing is possible (e.g. if one's liberty to smoke is much less important than one's liberty to participate in the political process, and the importance of the latter is comparable to the importance of some disutility which would be suffered by permitting the liberty to smoke, then the liberty to smoke is outweighed by its disutility).

Goods for which problems of accumulation can arise include those exhaustible by appropriation. But the problems are particularly severe, in contemporary Western society, for liquid assets and the so-called 'new forms of property' (e.g. management rights to corporate shares, pension funds, and trusts).[9] Accumulations of such wealth give the owners the power to influence political and social institutions to their advantage, and such advantages tend to snowball. Manipulation of the right of bequest is virtually useless as a way of dealing with the problem since trusts (and in the case of businesses, corporate management structures) are specifically designed to avoid the consequences of such manipulation. Revision of the tax system and what might be called 'personal anti-trust legislation' are the primary devices which must now be used when restrictions on the accumulation of property are called for. The details of specific and particular justification will be very complex, but at least the guidelines from the analysis of general justification are reasonably straightforward.

HARMFUL USE

The (Millean) labor theory will not justify any use of property which represents a loss to someone other than the owner. Liberty requires that the use owners make of their property not interfere with the liberty to which people are entitled. And utility prohibits uses which have a net disutility. The 'no harmful use' element of full, liberal ownership is therefore going to be a stringent one for goods which are dangerous. Use rights allowable for guns and pesticides, for example, are likely to be sharply limited. And in the case of hand guns, if significant disutility and loss of liberty to others is entailed by extensive private possession, it may be necessary to limit possession in order to satisfy the no harmful use requirement.[10]

Many restrictions on use imposed by the general justifications are identical with those alluded to under the headings of exhaustibility and accumulation. But use restrictions go beyond those others to provide, for example, a foundation for nuisance law and public safety law in cases where no problems of exhaustion or accumulation exist. The 'life before property' rule also finds a foundation here.[11]

The requirement of permitting maximal acquisition
Within the limits on ownership just discussed, the arguments from labor and liberty combine to produce a presumption in favor of allowing people to acquire full ownership (or whatever other variety they choose) of as much property as they want. Disutility significant enough to outweigh the labor and liberty arguments (assuming such balancing is morally permissible) can defeat the presumption, as can other considerations to be discussed below. But once the disutilities of exhaustibility, accumulation, and harmful use are taken care of, other disutilities serious enough to outweigh the labor and liberty arguments are likely to be rare — especially since most ownership which has an overall disutility also has some significant utility as well. Within the limits discussed, then, the general justifications support a presumption in favor of a system of private property which allows as much ownership as individuals choose to have.

The compensation requirement
Compensation becomes an issue in two contexts: in the acquisition of property rights and in their subsequent redefinition (by law).

THE ACQUISITION OF RIGHTS
For the former case, two principles from the general justifications are relevant. First, where an acquisition justifiably overrides a pre-existing right, compensation must be paid. (I assume acquisitions by *violations* of pre-existing rights — that is by *un*justifiable overridings — are not permissible.) Second, the desert form of the labor argument requires payment of a penalty to those who suffer a net loss from acquisitions by labor. I think enough has been said in previous chapters to suggest how those principles will work.

THE REDEFINITION OF RIGHTS AND REDISTRIBUTIVE JUSTICE
The problem of redefining rights, however, whether by taxation, restrictions on use, possession, bequest, and so on, has not been adequately discussed. I cannot give a detailed account here because the subject is so vast. But I can lay out the principles (arising from the analysis of general justification) which would guide a detailed account.

The problem is roughly this: the sorts of property rights which can be justified vary with social circumstances. Thus rights obtained justifiably in one time and place and perpetuated by justifiable transfers (and which are thus just in terms of what Nozick calls 'historical' considerations),[12] may turn out to be unjustifiable in terms of a good distribution for the current social situation. The problem is therefore what to do with rights whose acquisition was justifiable but whose continued existence is not. Possessors of such rights may argue that however the rights obtained from future acquisitions are defined, it is not permissible to make *post facto* changes in existing rights without the possessors' consent — no matter how unjustifiable they may have become. *Justice may both require a certain distributive result and prohibit the redistribution necessary to achieve it.* This is the crux of the problem raised by the (anti-property) argument from inequality.

There are at least two remedies for such conflicts. One is to obtain consent from the holders of 'anachronistic' rights for the necessary changes. The other is to make compensation to them in lieu of honoring their rights.[13] In many cases only partial changes in existing rights will need to be made anyway — changes in use rights only, and in alienability and transmissibility. More drastic changes can often wait for the first transfer. No doubt changes in the right of bequest would be unwelcome to the right-holders, yet it is important to note that the people who may be most poignantly and vociferously disappointed (i.e. prospective heirs) are *not* right-holders in any sense which can require compensation. At best they have merely recipient rights, and such rights cannot be 'cashed' here, because there are no persons 'against' whom the rights are held. Similarly, *mutatis mutandis*, for the prospective beneficiaries of transfers.

Changes in use rights and the rights of alienability can be crushing, and surely should be compensated.[14] Of course, where one can reasonably construe the right as having included from the outset the possibility of the changes (e.g. where the implied or express terms of the right are understood to be conditional on the existence of the social circumstances necessary for their justification) then no compensation is needed. But the temptation to read such a construction into all property rights *post facto* must be resisted. Surely justice requires at least that the test be one of what reasonable persons acquiring such rights, at the time they were acquired, would have understood them to be.

The relevant principles of redistributive justice are therefore these: (a) Where rights are anachronistic (i.e. justly acquired but no longer a justifiable part of the state of affairs), they must either be redefined with the consent of the holders, or if consent cannot be obtained, overridden with fair compensation given to the holders. (b) Redefinitions or overridings should be only those necessary to render the rights minimally justifiable for current holders, but maximally justifiable for future holders. (Example: where restrictive use rights need only be imposed on future owners, then they should not be imposed on current owners. Restrictions on what rights the present owners may transfer or transmit will be sufficient. But there is no reason to make the use rights acquirable by future owners the *minimally* justifiable ones. They should rather be the maximally justifiable ones. If it would be all right, all things considered, for future owners to have the right to do X and Y, but *best*, all things considered, if they only had the right to do X, then assuming the decision can be made by a legitimate social or political process, the rational decision must be for the best alternative. This might mean, in the case of the argument against the perpetuation of inequality, that a 'progressive' policy would be established — one in which current owners would be minimally disturbed, but in which sweeping changes in the system would be accomplished in stages by preventing transmissions and new acquisitions of the objectionable sorts.)

Two additional considerations

Aside from the limits imposed by the general justifications themselves, the justification of specific systems of property rights will of course have to take into account other relevant moral concerns. I cannot list all of them, but two are especially worthy of notice here.

THE PRESERVATION OF INDIVIDUAL AND PUBLIC VIRTUE

Ideals — for the sort of character traits which defines moral excellence in the person and for the sort of social institutions, pace, and variety of life which defines the ideal society — are important considerations in the specific justification of property rights. How competitive should a person be, ideally? How independent of others, economically? How mobile should people be? The sorts of ownership a system allows or encourages will have considerable influence on the nature of its social life, social organization, and on the character traits its people develop. Reform of property laws is quite rightly seen as a matter which could affect the dispositions to achieve, to work, to compete, to cooperate, and to give help to others; it could also influence the pace, mobility, complexity, and (for lack of a better word) humaneness of social life.[15] Utopian socialists exaggerate about the potential influence in one direction; utopian capitalists exaggerate about it in another. But the potential is there, and it must be given consideration in the course of the specific justification of property rights.

114

The source of ideals — the question of which ideals are morally justifiable — is an issue for the general theory of moral justification. Some philosophers argue that the virtues, or morally ideal character traits, are important mainly as means to the end of ensuring patterns of behavior which are on the whole valuable, or dutiful. Mill, for example, may be read as making the same sort of argument for roles or character traits as he did for rules or duties. And I have no doubt that Kant would have agreed that moral education, in this imperfect world, does as well to try to develop the inclination to respect the moral law as to develop the faculty of pure practical reason. I have argued elsewhere that virtues have a more fundamental place in moral argument than is usually (now) assigned to them — a place coordinate with values and obligations, in fact.[16] But even if that argument is not persuasive, it can be shown that inattention to ideals leads to oversights, misemphases, and other problems for moral justification.[17] The important point here is that the specific justification of property rights must confront these issues, however untidy and unmanageable they may seem.

THE PROBLEM OF CONSERVATION

The problem of saving for the distant future is a difficult one. (There are, of course, straightforward utility arguments available for saving for the *near* future.) Why should people living now sacrifice, or save, or improve and conserve things for those to be born two centuries from now? The answer is usually given in terms of the interests people have in making sure that at least the next generation is well off: they want to provide for their children, and they want to be well provided for when they can no longer do it for themselves. The overlapping of generations ensures a perpetual community of interests in saving for at least the probable life-span of the youngest existing members of society (or perhaps that of their probable children).

Further considerations extend the rationale for savings considerably. Assuming the probable life-span either remains constant or increases, and people continue to have children, the 'savings boundary' remains perpetually constant or becomes more distant. Thus, rather than constantly adjust the savings principle each year to accommodate the fact that the 'savings boundary' has come no closer, it may be more efficient to set up a rate of consumption, for renewable resources, which keeps the available level constant, and a rate of consumption for non-renewable resources vastly under what is required merely to provide for those who exist at the time given.

The way this is related to property rights is that, given the principle that one *should* save for the distant future, placing restrictions on accumulation and the right to bequeath may destroy some of the incentive for saving. This is, of course, an empirical question, but one which specific justification must face (assuming the principle of saving for the future is not abandoned altogether).

Probable directions for specific justification

The problems of specific justification are so complex that a single treatise like this — especially one which has already devoted considerable space to general justification — cannot possibly hope to do much more than indicate the general directions which changes in specific sorts of rights must take. Just to illustrate the complexities, consider mineral rights. To what extent should one allow them to be severed from title to (the surface of) the land? How should the boundaries of such rights be defined? By the surface boundaries extended downward? Or — as it is now by the so-called law of the apex — not only by the surface boundaries but also by the course of veins of a mineral which have their 'apex' within the surface boundaries, extended downward?[18] What use rights should be granted? What forms of original acquisition should be allowed? How should the relevant statutes be drawn?

The same level of complexity exists for water rights, land ownership, inheritance taxation, and 'non-corporeal' property (e.g. patents, copyrights, trademarks, etc.). Each requires a treatise of its own. But there are some general directions for all these areas which it may be useful to point out.

(1) Full, liberal ownership of land, at least in densely populated areas of industrialized societies, is a thing of the past. Use rights are already restricted by zoning ordinances, building codes, and planning boards. Whether this should be expanded or contracted, it certainly ought at least to be governed by a coherent and general set of policies, consistently applied.[19] Alienability and transmissibility rights may also have to be substantially revised to scale ownership down to life tenancies.

It should be noted, however, that measures appropriate for megalopolis are not necessarily appropriate for the remaining rural areas. In those areas, though land must, if scarce, be subject to restrictions on use, alienability, and transmissibility too, the purposes for which this needs to be done might well justify forms of ownership different from those justifiable for the cities.[20] One may wish to revive the doctrine of innocent use, for example, to provide public recreational space on what is otherwise private property. And though building codes may not need to be very restrictive in rural areas, the need for soil conservation and efficient crop management may require other stringent restrictions on use and capital rights.

(2) Ownership of vital depletable resources (fossil fuels, fresh water, mineral deposits) may have to be restricted to the rights of income, transfer, and limited transmissibility, with management, use, and actual possession effectively under public control. Again, this is a requirement (*if* it is a requirement) not of 'justice in the abstract,' but of the conditions imposed by general justification in a densely populated, industrial world in serious danger of exhausting its resources both by consumption and abuse. If the necessary conservation measures cannot be guaranteed (with any significant probability) under a system of full liberal ownership by individuals, then something along the outlines mentioned above seems the only rational course.

(3) Assuming that the preservation of a democratic political system is a moral necessity, new measures will have to be devised to limit accumulations. The present tax structure and the old rule against perpetuities[21] are not capable of preventing the accumulation of vast wealth in management, use, and transfer rights — wealth of the sort possessed by corporate boards, trustees, and the like; wealth which confers political power in quantities sufficient to undermine the democratic ideal.

These are some of the general directions it seems to me that a new theory of specific justification for property rights would have to take. Because the emphasis throughout this chapter has been rather heavy on restrictions to be imposed on owners, however, it may be useful to add two final, corrective reminders.

One is that the analysis of general justification has shown not only that private ownership is justifiable (in general), but that property rights may not be abridged, morally, without either the consent of the right-holder or compensation in lieu of that consent. Thus when anachronistic rights must be redefined, yet the holders' consent cannot be obtained and the society cannot make adequate compensation to them in lieu of honoring their rights, a high-level moral dilemma must be faced. It is a dilemma which revolutionary socialists tend to solve by simply overriding the rights, and which hard-line rights theorists tend to solve by ignoring the need for change. Neither solution is satisfactory. Consent must be obtained — and in an open society with a clear emergency, that may be possible with persistent, good-faith efforts. Or compensation must be paid — but if conventional payment cannot be made, nothing prohibits devising unconventional forms of compensation which *can* be made.

The other thing brought out by general justification is that private ownership is not only justifiable, but that the argument from liberty requires that the greatest extent of private ownership desired by an individual, and permitted by the general justifications, be allowed. If, within the constraints imposed by a crowded planet whose population is voraciously consuming its resources, this maximization principle has a hollow sound, then perhaps we should make more than empty gestures in the direction of changing population policies and wasteful life-styles.

Notes

Chapter 2   Property Rights

1   This typólogy – of rights, privileges, powers, and immunities – was
first expounded in a series of articles in the *Yale Law Journal*, collected in Wesley Newcomb Hohfeld, *Fundamental Legal Conceptions* (New Haven, Yale University Press, 1919). Hohfeld's
attempt to standardize legal usage was controversial from the start,
and while it is now highly regarded, has not been entirely successful.
Minor matters of nomenclature are still disputed (e.g. the substi-
tution of 'liberty' for 'privilege'). But more importantly, in the
pressures of practice, the precision Hohfeld hoped for often slips
away.

2   Hohfeld, *Fundamental Legal Conceptions*, pp. 36-64.

3   The characterizations of each type are my own but owe a good deal
to the clarity of the exposition in *Salmond on Jurisprudence*, 12th
edition (London, Sweet & Maxwell, 1966), §42, pp. 224-33.

4   Hohfeld uses simply 'right' here.

5   See L. J. Cohen, 'The Concept of Law,' *Mind*, LXXI: 395-412 (1962).

6   I follow Salmond's usage here, rather than using Hohfeld's term
'privilege.' Hohfeld himself admitted the appropriateness of 'liberty,'
but decided against it for reasons which have no force here. See
Hohfeld, *Fundamental Legal Conceptions*, pp. 46-8.

7   Hohfeld, *Fundamental Legal Conceptions*, pp. 50-1.

8   Not to be confused with the 'rights of recipience' spoken of in
D. D. Raphael and B. Mayo, 'Human Rights,' *Proceedings of the
Aristotelean Society, Supplementary Volume*, XXXIX: 205-36
(1965).

9   Whether one can say that there are *legal* recipient rights is an
interesting question. The law is (rightly) reluctant to recognize
unenforceable rights-relationships, and in so far as duty-bearers
cannot be specified for them it is hard to see how recipient rights
could be enforced. But talk about such rights may lead to legislation

which upgrades them to claim rights by specifying duty-bearers.
They thus have a direct bearing on the law.

10 H. L. A. Hart, *The Concept of Law* (Oxford, Clarendon Press, 1961),
pp. 163-76.

11 It has been given both broader and narrower meanings, however.
Writers like Blackstone, Hobbes, and Locke occasionally used it to
refer to all a person's legal rights — to whatever was one's in law —
a usage which has been the source of some confusion. In law the
term also sometimes refers only to proprietary rights *in rem* as
opposed to proprietary rights *in personam* (that is, to those ownership rights one has 'against the world' as opposed to those one has
against specified persons). The former is the province of property
law; the latter, contract law. 'Property' has even been restricted so
far as to refer only to the rights of ownership in material objects. See,
for a review of these uses, *Salmond on Jurisprudence*, 12th edition,
pp. 411-12, and compare the relevant entries in *Black's Law
Dictionary*, 4th edition (Minneapolis, West Publishing Co., 1968).
In systems uninfluenced by Roman law, the notion of property is
apparently understood mainly as physical possession rather than as
what we would call the rights of ownership. See the discussion and
references in J. C. Smith, 'The Concept of Native Title,' *University
of Toronto Law Journal,* 24: 1 at 6 (1974). These variants are
important to keep in mind when reading discussions of property,
but I shall, as I say, adhere to the more conventional identification
of property rights with the rights of ownership *per se* — that is,
proprietary rights *in rem* and *in personam,* over corporeal or non-
corporeal things. Where such distinctions become important, I shall
call attention to them.

12 This is true of both the classic sources and very recent accounts.
See, for example, Frank Snare, 'The Concept of Property,' *American
Philosophical Quarterly*, 9: 200-7 (1972).

13 A. M. Honoré, 'Ownership' in *Oxford Essays in Jurisprudence,*
A. G. Guest (ed.) (Oxford, Clarendon Press, 1961), pp. 107-47.

14 This is perhaps a disputable case. But the person who has the right
to manage a union pension fund, or the vast assets of a mutual
fund, certainly has something which others treat as wealth or
property. And the accumulation of such management rights poses
something of a problem for property law reformers. See John W.
VanDoren, 'Redistributing Wealth by Curtailing Inheritance,'
Florida State University Law Review, 3: 33-63 (1975).

15 'The Finality of Moral Judgements,' *Philosophical Review,* LXXXII:
364-70 (1973).

Chapter 3 The Argument from First Occupancy

1 See Cicero, *On Ends,* book III, xx, 67; and Seneca, *On Benefits,*
book VII, xii, 3.

2 Samuel Pufendorf, *De Jure Naturae et Gentium,* translation of 1688 edition by C. H. and W. A. Oldfather (Oxford, Clarendon Press, 1934), book IV, iv, 2-6.
3 J.-J. Rousseau, *The Social Contract* (New York, E. P. Dutton, 1959), book I, chapter ix, pp. 20-1. It should be remarked that the requirement of actual or effective occupation has been generally followed throughout the history of the appropriation of the earth's land resources — at least from 'The Age of Discovery' on. See, for an interesting review of the relevant legal history, McDougall, Lasswell, Vlasic, and Smith, 'The Enjoyment and Acquisition of Resources in Outer Space,' *University of Pennsylvania Law Review,* 111: 521 at 611 ff. (1963).
4 Immanuel Kant, *The Metaphysics of Morals, Part I: The Metaphysical Elements of Justice,* translated by John Ladd (Indianapolis, Bobbs-Merrill, 1965), pp. 44-56. In the Königliche Preussische Akademie der Wissenschaft edition of Kant's works, the relevant passages are found in volume VI at 237-46.
5 G. W. F. Hegel, *Philosophy of Right,* translated by T. M. Knox (Oxford, Clarendon Press, 1942), pp. 37-41.
6 For a recent attempt to use the notion of first appropriation in these ways, see Robert LeFevre, *The Philosophy of Ownership* (Colorado, Pine Tree Publications, 1966), pp. 34-42.
7 Consider Rousseau's remarks in *The Social Contract,* book I, chapter ix, pp. 19-22.

Chapter 4 The Labor Theory of Property Acquisition

1 For a review of the relevant history, see Richard Schlatter, *Private Property: The History of an Idea* (New Brunswick, N.J., Rutgers University Press, 1951). I do not mean to say, of course, that the idea was unknown outside state-of-nature theory. The Romans, who gave it no legal force at all, did in practice sometimes recognize it in the case of sons who could not formally own property at all; what they produced on their own was occasionally treated by the *paterfamilias* as their (the sons') own. See Barry Nicholas, *An Introduction to Roman Law* (Oxford, Clarendon Press, 1962), p. 68.
2 Marx, for example, never explicitly denies that laborers are entitled in justice to the fruits of their labor. (Indeed, it is natural to think that his condemnation of capitalist exploitation depends on a conviction that laborers are entitled to the *whole* fruits of their labor.) He is scornful of the theory of primitive acquisition. See *Capital,* vol. I, part VIII, chapter xxvi as translated from the third and revised from the fourth German editions (Chicago, Charles H. Ken, 1924). And the root idea of the labor theory seems inconsistent with the communism which is to result from the classless society in which labor has become unalienated. But I can find no place in which he specifically attacks the idea.

3 In the Second of *Two Treatises on Government*. All references will be to the standard numbered paragraphs of this work.

4 My attention was called to this problem by David Ozar's paper, 'Locke's Labor Theory of Property,' presented at the Western Division Meetings of the American Philosophical Association, 1975.

5 Robert Nozick, *Anarchy, State and Utopia* (New York, Basic Books, 1974), pp. 174-5.

6 See Henry George, *Progress and Poverty* (New York, Henry Schalkenbach Foundation, 1955), reprint of the 1905 edition, p. 337.

7 See J. S. Mill, *Principles of Political Economy* in *The Collected Works of John Stuart Mill*, volume II (London, Routledge & Kegan Paul, 1965), book II, 1, §3 (p. 208).

8 The legal status and extent of such rights is currently under some strain — and therefore a topic of discussion — due to the rise of organ transplantation. The law has long forbidden the pledging or selling of body parts by their 'owners' (while in some places permitting the sale of blood and sperm). But for a recent argument for a change in the law, see 'The Sale of Human Body Parts,' *Michigan Law Review*, 72: 1182-264 (1974).

9 P. J. Proudhon, *What is Property?* [originally published in 1867] (New York, Howard Fertig, 1966), p. 61.

10 *Salmond on Jurisprudence*, 12th edition (London, Sweet & Maxwell, 1966), chapter 13.

11 Hugo Grotius, *De Jure Belli ac Pacis*, translation of 1646 edition by F. W. Kelsey and others (Oxford, Clarendon Press, 1926), book II, chapter III, §IV, no. 1. The reader may also find Socrates' arguments about his status as a child of the Laws interesting in this connection. (I refer to the arguments against civil disobedience in Plato's *Crito*.) Contrast this with Aristotle's remark in *Nichomachean Ethics* (book V, chapter 6, at 1134b). And, of course, while Greek law was apparently less than literal in its treatment of children as chattels, early Roman law was very literal indeed about it. See Nicholas, *An Introduction to Roman Law*, pp. 65 ff. The *paterfamilias* could lawfully kill, as well as sell, *a filius familias* at his discretion — apparently as late as the second century A.D. Nor could a *filius familias* own property in law, though the custom was to let him use the produce of his labor as if it were his property. Only upon the death of one's father (supposing one had not been sold into slavery or emancipated) did a son become himself a *paterfamilias* and property owner.

12 *Ibid.,* book II, chapter II, §VI-X.

13 George, *Progress and Poverty*, p. 347.

14 Proudhon, *What is Property?*, p. 84.

15 Mill, *Principles of Political Economy*, book II, chapter 2, §6 (page 230). The passage continues, with respect to land, 'But it is some

hardship to be born into the world and to find all nature's gifts previously engrossed, and no place left for the newcomer.' For a recent discussion which closely parallels Mill – especially with regard to the 'no loss' requirement – see George I. Mavrodes, 'Property,' *Personalist,* 53: 245-62 (1972).

16 What is required by morality is, broadly, what one is justifiably liable for reprobation for not doing (though one may not usually demand *approbation* for *doing* it). What is not required, but merely permitted or encouraged, is what one can*not* be liable for reprobation for not doing, and for doing which one ought to get approbation. The requirements of morality are generally expressed as duties or obligations. This is harmless enough as long as one does not overlook the character traits whose absence makes a person subject to reproof (as opposed merely to the absence of positive endorsements), and the times when a failure to choose the *best* available alternative (as opposed to one which is merely adequate) also makes the agent subject to sanction.

17 Locke, *Second Treatise,* paragraph 34.

18 Hastings Rashdall, 'The Philosophical Theory of Property,' in J. V. Bartlett (ed.), *Property: Its Duties and Rights,* 2nd edition (London, Macmillan, 1915), pp. 54-6.

19 Nozick makes interesting remarks on these issues in *Anarchy, State and Utopia* (New York, Basic Books, 1974), at pp. 141 and 182. See also Ayn Rand, 'Patents and Copyrights,' in her *Capitalism: The Unknown Ideal* (New York, New American Library, 1966), pp. 125-9. For a review of current legal theory on intellectual property, see the Note by Joseph E. Kovacs, 'Beyond the Realm of Copyright: Is There Legal Sanctuary for the Merchant of Ideas?' *Brooklyn Law Review,* 41: 284 (1974).

20 A word needs to be said here about thought-experiments in ethics. State-of-nature imagery is sometimes compared to notions in the physical sciences such as uniform motion. Uniform motion is an imaginary phenomenon, but useful for the foundation of an explanatory and predictive account of motion as it actually occurs in experience. Similarly, it is said, though no state of nature exists (or probably ever did exist), the concept can help construct a justification for states of affairs which actually do or could exist. The parallel is plausible, but dangerous. Motion exists. Uniform motion is a linear extrapolation to the vanishing point, as it were, of certain properties of real motion. To the extent that the notion of a state of nature is similarly an extrapolation, the parallel looks sound. But when it turns out that *only* in the 'unreal' conditions can a given type of social arrangement be justified (e.g. private ownership of all available land), then the use of the imaginary situation in moral theory becomes something of a menace to clear thinking.

21 I am indebted to Robert Nozick and Ruth Barcan Marcus for providing the stimulus to my reflections on this line of argument.

22 Joel Feinberg, 'Justice and Personal Desert,' in his book *Doing and Deserving* (Princeton University Press, 1970), pp. 55-87.

23 *Ibid.*, p. 58.

24 *Ibid.*, pp. 58-9.

25 *Ibid.*, pp. 58-9.

26 One must be very careful here not to slip into saying that one who deserves X is *entitled* to it — where 'entitled' means 'has a claim right.' People may deserve things which they have no claim right to (i.e. which others have no duty to provide); and they may have claim rights to things which they do not deserve. Desert must also be distinguished from eligibility. See Feinberg, 'Justice and Personal Desert., pp. 58-9.

27 *Ibid.*, pp. 62 ff. Feinberg distinguishes contexts in which desert is a 'polar' concept (e.g. reward and punishment contexts) from those in which it is not (e.g. deserving the trophy for winning the race). He would, I think, agree that in the context under discussion here, desert was necessarily polar. In an appendix to his article (*ibid.*, pp. 88-94), Feinberg discusses economic benefits as deserved, and concludes that they are best regarded (if deserts at all) as compensations. But he does not consider arguments of the form I shall advance here.

28 Suppose we used a different principle of desert — one which said people deserved something (benefit for effort? penalty for ineptitude?) for *un*productive labor as well as for productive labor. Then would the proportionality requirement look like this?

> benefit = value of labor + value of labor's product;
> penalty = value (disvalue?) of labor + disvalue of labor's product.

Compare Nozick's suggestions for a retributive principle for punishment in *Anarchy, State and Utopia*, pp. 59-63.

29 James D. Watson, *The Double Helix* (New York, Mentor Books, 1968).

30 Of course, the other's kindness may itself be inappropriate, but that raises a separate issue.

Chapter 5   Arguments from Utility

1 Mill says 'Private property, as an institution, did not owe its origin to any of those considerations of utility which plead for the maintenance of it when established.' He clearly thinks that 'originally,' people simply took things and kept them. Civil society grew up as a way of repressing violence. Property law was part of what was

required to do that. *Principles of Political Economy,* II, 1, §2 (p. 201). Harold Demsetz, 'Toward a Theory of Property Rights,' *American Economic Review, Proceedings and Papers,* 57: 347-59 (1967) suggests the contrary, however, for the economic variety of utility arguments.

2 I have addressed the problems of moral scepticism in previous writings — specifically Becker, *On Justifying Moral Judgments* (London, Routledge & Kegan Paul; New York, Humanities Press, 1973).

3 David Hume, *Treatise of Human Nature* (ed.) Selby-Bigge (Oxford, Clarendon Press, 1960), book III, part II, §II (pp. 484-5).

4 *Ibid.,* pp. 487-8.

5 *Ibid.*

6 John Locke, *Second Treatise of Government,* paragraph 28.

7 Aristotle, *Politics,* book II, chapter 5 [at 1263a] in Richard McKeon, (ed.), *The Basic Works of Aristotle* (New York, Random House, 1941), p. 1151.

8 G. W. F. Hegel, *Philosophy of Right,* §41.

9 See, for example, T. H. Green, *Principles of Political Obligation* (Ann Arbor, University of Michigan Press, 1967), chapter IV.

10 Hugo Grotius, *De Jure Belli ac Pacis,* II, II, XI.

11 Becker, *op. cit.*

12 These two modes of measurement typically yield different conclusions about the value of a thing to a person. See E. J. Mishan, 'Welfare Criteria for External Effects,' *American Economic Review,* 51: 541-613 at 602-3. Arguments which rely on one of these measures to the exclusion of the other are likely to be significantly biased. See the criticism of Posner's *Economic Analysis of Law* in C. Edwin Baker, 'The Ideology of the Economic Analysis of Law,' *Philosophy and Public Affairs,* 5: 3-48 (Autumn 1975).

13 For a presentation of this argument, see Harold Demsetz, 'Toward a Theory of Property Rights,' *American Economic Review, Proceedings and Papers,* 57: 347-59 (1967).

14 Richard A. Posner, *Economic Analysis of Law* (Boston, Little Brown, 1972), chapter 2.

15 For an explanation of this concept, rather new in economics, see Paul A. Samuelson, *Economics,* 9th edition (New York, McGraw Hill, 1973), pp. 195 ff.

16 See Oskar Lange, 'On the Economic Theory of Socialism,' in the book of the same title edited by B. E. Lippincott (Minneapolis, University of Minnesota Press, 1966) reprinted in part in Bruce A. Ackerman, *Economic Foundations of Property Law* (Boston, Little Brown, 1975), pp. 69-76.

17 Frank I. Michelman, 'Property, Utility and Fairness: Comments on the Ethical Foundations of 'Just Compensation Law,' *Harvard Law Review,* 80: 1165 at 1173 (1967).

18 One of the standard examples is R. H. Coase, 'The Problem of Social Cost,' *Journal of Law and Economics,* 3: 1-44 (1960).

19 See Robert C. Ellickson, 'Alternatives to Zoning: Covenants, Nuisance Rules, and Fines as Land Use Controls,' *University of Chicago Law Review,* 40: 681 (1973) reprinted in part in Ackerman, *Economic Foundations of Property Law,* pp. 265-307.

20 See Guido Calabresi, 'The Decision for Accidents: An approach to Non-Fault Allocation of Costs,' *Harvard Law Review,* 78: 713 (1965); 'Fault, Accidents and the Wonderful World of Blum and Kalven,' *Yale Law Journal,* 75: 216 (1965).

21 E.g. Jacob H. Beuscher and Rober R. Wright (eds.) *Land Use: Cases and Materials,* 5th edition (St Paul, West Publishing Co., 1969).

22 See the examples in R. H. Coase, 'The Problem of Social Cost,' *Journal of Law and Economics,* 3: 1-44 (1960).

23 C. Edwin Baker, 'Utility and Rights: Two Justifications for State Action Increasing Equality,' *Yale Law Journal,* 84: 39 (1974) makes arguments of this sort. And for general comments on the inadequacy of economic utility arguments, taken *alone,* at the level of specific justification, see Guido Calabresi and A. Douglas Melamed, 'Property Rules, Liability Rules and Inalienability.' *Harvard Law Review,* 85: 1089 (1972).

24 See *Hadacheck* v. *Sebastian,* 239 US 394 (1915).

Chapter 6 The Argument from Political Liberty

1 John Rawls, *A Theory of Justice* (Cambridge, Harvard University Press, 1971). For impassioned argument fragments to the effect that the right to life (a liberty right) entails claim rights to property, see Ayn Rand, 'Man's Rights,' in her *Capitalism: The Unknown Ideal* (New York, New American Library, 1966), pp. 287-94.

2 For example, Mill in *On Liberty* and Rawls, in *A Theory of Justice.*

3 Robert Nozick's arguments against anarchism in *Anarchy, State and Utopia* (New York, Basic Books, 1974) seem to me to be as conclusive as philosophical arguments can get on this issue.

4 Harry W. Jones, for example, summarizing the state of the law in 1962, says it is fair to say that US law generally holds that 'an enterpriser's freedom from government compulsion must yield whenever . . . a reasonable legislator would be justified in concluding that the restraint imposed is an appropriate one to improve the economic opportunity of far larger numbers of people.' Harry W. Jones, 'Freedom and Opportunity as Compelling Social Values,' *NOMOS,* IV: pp. 227-42, at 235 (1962).

Chapter 7 Considerations of Moral Character

1 See the relevant history in R. B. Schlatter, *Private Property: The History of an Idea* (New Brunswick, N.J., Rutgers University Press,

1951) and Bartlett (ed.), *Property: Its Duties and Rights,* 2nd edition (London, Macmillan, 1915).
2   Aristotle, *Politics,* book II, chapter 5, at 1263b.

Chapter 8   Anti-Property Arguments

1   Some people who make what amounts to the disutility argument: Plato (for the guardians only); Rousseau in *Discourse on the Origins of Inequality*; Proudhon in *What is Property?*; Henry George in *Progress and Poverty*; and Marx in *Capital.*
2   That is, not only the elements of personality which must be present for one to survive physically or to maintain a reasonably comfortable existence, but the ones — like the capacity for aesthetic appreciation, the habits of reflective thought, and the delight in play and sport — which require some leisure and security for their development.
3   See, for a discussion and bibliography on the cardinality problem, Nicholas Resher, *Distributive Justice* (Indianapolis, Bobbs-Merrill, 1966), chapter 2.
4   Rashdall, 'The Philosophical Theory of Property,' in Bartlett, *Property: Its Duties and Rights,* pp. 45-6.
5   Plato, *Republic,* book II.
6   See the review of Christian positions in Bartlett, *op. cit.*
7   I am indebted to Professor Ted Honderich and to Mr David Godwin for pressing me to examine this argument.
8   Ted Honderich, 'On Inequality and Violence, and the Differences We Make between Them,' in R. S. Peters (ed.), *Nature and Conduct,* Royal Institute of Philosophy Lectures, volume 8, 1973-4 (London, Macmillan, 1975), pp. 46-82.

Chapter 9   The Justification of Property Rights

1   See, for a summary of existing evidence on these matters, Edward O. Wilson, *Sociobiology* (Cambridge, Harvard University Press, 1975). Material relating especially to space is presented informally in Edward T. Hall, *The Hidden Dimension* (New York, Doubleday, 1966). Hall discusses distinctions between 'flight distance,' 'critical distance,' personal and social distance, 'sociofugal' and 'sociopetal' spaces, among others. Some special properties of the envelopes of space 'appropriated' by a person are discussed by Gordon Allport in his book *Becoming* (New Haven, Yale University Press, 1955). And of course the subject has not been ignored in literature — even comic poetry:

> Some thirty inches from my nose
> The frontier of my Person goes,
> And all the untilled air between
> Is private *pagus* or desmesne.

> Stranger, unless with bedroom eyes
> I beckon you to fraternize,
> Beware of rudely crossing it:
> I have no gun, but I can spit.
> W. H. Auden,
> 'Prologue: The Birth of Architecture.'

2 I have advanced detailed arguments for a schema of moral justification which relies on species characteristics as presumptive criteria for grounding judgments of value, of obligation, and of virtue in *On Justifying Moral Judgments.*

3 Rawls, *A Theory of Justice*, §39 and §82.

4 Nozick, *Anarchy, State and Utopia*, pp. 28-35.

5 For more detail on these matters, see my *On Justifying Moral Judgments*, chapter XIX, and 'The Neglect of Virtue,' *Ethics:* 85 110-22 (1975).

6 For a recent legal writing on this topic, see Lynton K. Caldwell, 'Rights of Ownership or Rights of Use? – The Need for a New Conceptual Basis for Land Use Theory,' *William and Mary Law Review*, 15: 759 (1974); and Donald W. Large. 'This Land is Whose Land? Changing Concepts of Land as Property,' *Wisconsin Law Review*, 1039-83 (1973); and McDougall, Lasswell, Vlasic and Smith, 'The Enjoyment and Acquisition of Resources in Outer Space,' *University of Pennsylvania Law Review,* 111: 521 at pp. 575 ff. (1963). The last is particularly helpful.

7 An interesting attempt to deal with this is Frank E. Maloney *et al.*, *A Model Water Code, With Commentary* (Gainsville, University of Florida Press, 1972). For a critique, see Frank J. Trelease, 'The Model Water Code, The Wise Administrator, and the Goddam Bureaucrat,' *Natural Resources Journal*, 14: 207-29 (1974).

8 For a discussion of some aspects of the current problem here, see John W. VanDoren, 'Redistributing Wealth by Curtailing Inheritance,' *Florida State University Law Review*, 3: 33-63 (1975).

9 *Ibid.*, p. 33, n. 2.

10 The case law on the no harmful use doctrine is fascinating. For a start, the reader might compare *Pennsylvania Coal Co.* v. *Sanderson* 113 Pa. 126, 6A. 453 (1886) in which a coal mining company was given the right virtually to destroy a stream; and *Just* v. *Marinette County* 56 Wisc. 2nd 7, 201 N.W.2^d 761 (1972) in which an individual landowner was fined for filling in a marshy area near a lake without a permit.

11 I refer, here, to the rule in tort law that one may, without legal liability in tort, damage another's property to save a life, but not to save one's property. See William J. Prosser, *Torts*, 4th edition (Minneapolis, West Publishing Co., 1971), pp. 124 ff.

12 Nozick, *Anarchy, State and Utopia*, chapter 7. A related but more complicated problem arises when one social system which

recognizes property rights becomes 'servient' to another – as when a colonial power takes over inhabited lands. Then the dominant system must deal with problems of 'native title.' See J. C. Smith, 'The Concept of Native Title,' *University of Toronto Law Review,* 24: 1 (1974).

13 Property rights are protected by the United States Constitution against expropriation 'without due process of law.' See the Fifth and Fourteenth Amendments. But the interesting legal issue is deciding when the state's exercise of its 'police power' in regulating the *use* of property has become a 'constructive taking' – a *de facto* expropriation for which compensation must be paid. For comments and references, see Donald W. Large, 'This Land is Whose Land?' p. 1048. My view is that since security in use is a version of ownership, and thus use rights are property rights, *all* changes in them should get constitutional protection. Consent should be gotten from owners or compensation should be paid. This position would be regarded by some legal theorists as unworkably stringent. See Frank I. Michelman, 'Property, Utility and Fairness,' *Harvard Law Review,* 80: 1165-258 (1968), and Joseph L. Sax, 'Takings, Private Property and Public Rights,' *Yale Law Journal,* 81: 149-86 (1971).

14 See the astonishing (and mercifully unused) case of *Hadacheck* v. *Sebastian* 239 US 394 (1915) in which a city was allowed to change a zoning ordinance, wiping out a man's fortune, without paying compensation.

15 A recent article which outlines the arguments for a free market system approach to the sale of human body parts (by their 'owners') ignores this sort of problem almost entirely. Yet I think it is the most potent source of likely objection to such a proposal. See 'The Sale of Human Body Parts,' *Michigan Law Review,* 72: 1182-264 (1972).

16 *On Justifying Moral Judgments,* chapter II.

17 See my 'The Neglect of Virtue.'

18 John L. Neff, 'The Law of the Apex,' *Rocky Mountain Mineral Law Institute,* 18: 387-414.

19 There is some interesting literature on alternatives to zoning. Houston, Texas (an unzoned city with special powers to enforce privately drawn restrictive covenants) has been studied by Bernard H. Siegan, 'Non-Zoning in Houston,' *Journal of Law and Economics,* 13: 71 (1970). And Robert C. Ellickson, 'Alternatives to Zoning: Covenants, Nuisance Rules, and Fines as Land Use Controls,' *University of Chicago Law Review,* 40: 681-781 (1973) is very helpful here.

20 Going farther afield, some who have considered the problems for the justification of property rights arising from space exploration have suggested that 'exclusive appropriation' (i.e. the acquisition of exclusive possessory, use, and capital rights) may be ruled out

(by joint agreement) except for certain stock resources. See McDougall, Lasswell, Vlasic and Smith, 'The Enjoyment and Acquisition of Resources in Outer Space.'

21 For a brief and illuminating definition of the rule against perpetuities, its rationale, and how it differs from various other devices for restricting alienability, see J. H. C. Morris and W. Barton Leach, *The Rule Against Perpetuities,* 2nd edition (London, Stevens, 1962), chapter 1. It is there pointed out that the rule is really not against alienability *per se* (because trustees may sell and buy securities for a trust), but rather a rule against too remote a vesting of interests. The most plausible rationale for the rule seems to be that 'It is a natural human desire to provide for one's family in the forseeable future. The difficulty is that if one generation is allowed to create unlimited future interests in property, succeeding generations will receive the property in a restricted state and be unable to indulge the same desire.' Morris and Leach, *The Rule Against Perpetuities,* p. 17. Without such a rule, property rights would be subject to the self-defeatingness objection.

Index